ACNOW

I would like t

the help and support they

me in writing this book and by letting me use their names were appropriate. My husband, John has been a rock giving his solid support and backing. My long-suffering daughters and husbands who have listened to me patiently while I've chatted on about my plans and sorted out my computer when I've pressed a wrong button. Especially my best friend Judith who had listened to my woes for too many years to remember and cousin Jillian who so patiently proof read every word for me.

I also must thank all my B&B guests, especially those who haven't had a mention because they were the 'easy' customers who made my life easy. I hope you all enjoy the book.

FORWARD

Farming and tourism have long been "bedfellows" and this witty memoire from Mary is a delight to read as she interweaves local folklore and culture with the development of cutting edge international companies and ancient history with tales of the trials, tribulations and darn-right pleasure of bringing up a family whilst operating a living farm and B&B.

In addition to Farming and Tourism Mary has played leading roles in education and the wider business community. Chairing many organisations, including both Delyn and Flintshire Tourism Associations. She draws on an unrivalled deep reservoir of understanding of and sensitivity to, how the riches of the landscape, rivers, sea and subterranean treasures have impacted on the lives of those living in the areas towns and villages. Her compassion for the people who live and visit along with her strong desire to share local knowledge, provide a hearty, warm Welsh welcome comes shining through.

If you have visited Flintshire and North East Wales this book will bring back many happy memories and enthuse you to return. If you have yet to visit I'm sure you will be inspired to discover this wonderful part of Wales that has been Mary's home.

Adrian Barsby
Chair Wales Tourism Alliance

This must-read little book is incredibly interesting from a number of perspectives. The author was and is clearly passionate and dedicated to everything she does, and we get a wonderful insight, over a few decades, about how to run a B&B and about local history - there's such a lot in the book to identify with for both the people of North Wales and for those who have visited the area as a tourist. Mary's stories had me giggling, laughing, gasping, shocked and almost crying. She writes from the heart about spotting an opportunity, adapting to new circumstances (including a growing family and a changing climate for tourism), about humour, joy, loss, friendship, love - and more. I highly recommend 'Full house'.

Jillian Rothwell

FULL HOUSE
GREENHILL CAPERS

CONTENT

CHAPTER 1
INTRODUCTION

In the spring of 1975 I decided I needed to find an income to supplement the farm income. With two children under five years old and myself being needed as the 'third hand' on the farm my options where limited. The 'third hand' is that moment when two people are needed to do some jobs such as moving cattle. Cattle know if there is only one of you trying to drive them through a gate or into a pen and they will just run back and to, when the 'third hand' arrives they know they can't do this and will go straight where you want them to go. I'd heard about another farmer's wife who had done Bed and Breakfast and, as we lived within walking distance of St. Winfried's Holy Well, Holywell, in what was then Flintshire; it seemed like a good idea. We later became Clwyd and then went back to Flintshire although we didn't move house at all. We also had an incredible view over the Wirral peninsular and could see as far away as Blackpool, with the Pepsi Max Big One ride next to it, on a clear day. With such a beautiful view and the nearest beach only about 5 miles away at Talacre and there was plenty for guests to do in the area visiting the Well and at that time, the Military Museum in the Caves up the road. These caves were man made and had stored the famous bouncing bombs invented by Barnes Wallis during the Second World War and immortalised in the popular Dambusters film. They had been converted into a military museum and I had donated my old food ration cards to be displayed; now I'm showing my age although rationing lasted well into the nineteen fifties. It had built up quite a following and was a popular attraction but they had a problem when a mine shaft collapsed closing their road and then when they built the A55 duel carriageway and the traffic through Holywell reduced considerably. They had built their trade on a sign at the end of the road but they couldn't get planning permission for signs on the A55 and sadly they eventually went out of business.

The view from Greenhill Farm must be seen to be believed. You can stand at the front of the house and look down onto the River Dee where once the Vikings rowed in to rape and pillage the local population. It is now quite silted up and has to be dredged regularly so that the plane wings built at British Aerospace can be taken down on barges to Mostyn Docks to be shipped to Toulouse in France for assembly. Before it silted up ferries ran from Greenfield to Liverpool from where people could get a ship to anywhere in the world. From the farm you look over the Wirral peninsular with Hilbre Island at the end. This is an outcrop of sandstone and the only rocky outcrop for seals etc to stop on between Llandudno and Cumbria. You can also see the Wirral Country Park and Parkgate. People still visit Parkgate as it is a port looking out over marshland; it's a real oddity to walk down the quayside looking at grass. On very high spring tides the water will cover the marshes. Over the top of this lies the Liverpool sky line with its cathedral towers standing out. Further still you can see the sand shining on Southport beach and even Blackpool tower with the Pepsi Max ride on the Pleasure Beach next to it. In the winter, when it's snows you can see the outline of the Cumbrian hills. That's if you want to stand outside long enough as the wind can be bitter in the winter. I always said that you knew when spring was coming as you stopped to see if the tide was in or out, you really didn't care when the weather was bad.

From the back of the house the view looks across our fields and up towards Brynford mountain, another oddity as it is owned by the Duke of Westminster. It is a site of special interests as it has some rare plants and butterflies, people have grazing rights on the mountain for their sheep allotted according to the acreage they own, it is an urban common giving anyone rights to walk over it and there are also quarrying rights. Underneath it there are lead mines with small shafts sunk into the ground which occasionally collapse and have to be capped.

The Catholic shrine, St. Winifred's Holy Well, although little heard of in the UK, is a thousand years older than Lourdes in France. It sits above Basingwerk Abbey, which was founded by Ranulf do Gernon, 4th Earl of Chester in 1132 when he brought in Benedictine monks from Normandy. It later became part of the Cistercian order. The abbey is now a shell of its former self. When Henry VIII dissolved the monasteries and took over their properties he did a deal with the then Abbott who kept some of the lands, these are now owned by the Mostyn Estates. Our farm was formally on the Mostyn Estates but it was sold off in the early 1900's to pay death duty along with other properties in the area. We could never prove it but we thought Greenhill was originally the Lower Grange Farm for the Abbey. The Middle and

Upper Grange farmers have been identified but not the Lower Grange. A monastic grange was a manor or an outlying farm belonging to a monastery worked by the monks to provide food for themselves and their visitors.

The story of St Winifred is quite gruesome. She rejected a suitor called Cardoc and so he cut her head off, it rolled down the hill and when it stopped St. Beuno lifted it up, put it back on her head and restored her to life. She became a nun and is buried in Shrewsbury Abbey. A spring started to flow from the spot where she was killed and from that time on the waters were visited and taken as a cure for all ailments. St. Winifred's Well is now surrounded by a chapel with the, Church of Wales, church above it and the more modern Catholic Church above that. The first written mention of people visiting the well was in 1115. It has enjoyed royal patronage over the years; it was visited by Henry V in 1415, Edward 1V in 1461 and Henry V11 before he became king in 1485. The last 'healing' was in the 1970's. It is still visited by over 2,000 people a year and in June every year a special service is held to commemorate St Winifred. People meet in the Catholic Church, situated above the Church of Wales, and walk down to the Well where a service of remembrance is held. To take the 'cure' you have to walk down the steps into the waters, which is about waist deep, cross the waters and up the steps on the other side three times. The water is cold, I haven't taken the cure but I have felt the waters. My grandmother told me she visited the well as a child, because her grandmother had retired near by, and it was surrounded by deserted crutches. These have now been removed, on 'health and safety' grounds.

With so much of interest to see and do locally I thought there must be a need for accommodation. I had no experience of running any sort of accommodation facility but I had stayed in hotels and I thought I knew enough to get by. After doing my A levels at school I had gone on to the Domestic and Trades College in Manchester to study Management for the Clothing industry and so I had some management skills. It was much easier to start a business in those days, all we really had to do was put a sign at the end of the road. When we are young we think we can 'do it all' with no thoughts of any problems we may find on our journey through life.

The farmhouse was huge; in the 1700's it had been an Inn where the local gentry came to dine and then walk down to Holywell's Bowling Green. This is mentioned in a book called The History of the Parishes of Whitford and Holywell, written by a local journalist and travel writer, Thomas Pennant in 1796. He called it 'The House of Bryn Celyn', but as it is the only house above the Bowing Green it has to be Greenhill. Bryn Celyn is a small hamlet of about 40 houses above which the farm stands overlooking the Greenfield Valley which in the 1700's had mills built along its length taking advantage of the stream to run over water wheels to give power. It had the unenviable reputation of being where copper bracelets were made to ship across to Liverpool and then on to Africa to exchange for people who were sent to America to work on the plantations. Bryn Celyn translates from the Welsh as 'Holly Hill' and my in-laws had sold Holly from the woods the first Christmas they had moved in as it grew prolifically in the area. Beer was brewed in the cellar and originally there was a malting room. In 1945, when my in-laws moved there, it was a house and 4 flats. It had no running water or inside toilets. It was condemned by the council and the tenants moved into council houses in the 1960's. My husband, John's mother and father bought the farm and put running water and a bathroom into their side of the house. By 1975 it was split into two parts. My in-laws lived in one side and my husband, John, myself and our two small daughters, Susan and Jennifer, lived in the other side. The house was so big that there where 4 empty rooms in the middle, two upstairs and 2 downstairs. The downstairs rooms where used for storage. The room at the back had an outside door into it and so was used to store the potatoes and eggs we sold on our milk round. This room had a stone slab floor but also had a cellar underneath it. One morning John walked into the room carrying a bag of potatoes and when straight through the floor into the cellar. He was lucky he wasn't badly hurt, he was just bruised. It turned out that the original floor was wood and the heavy stone slabs had just been laid on top of it. It was a strange old house built in various periods. My in-laws lived in the oldest part and we were in the 'newer' part built in the late seventeen or early eighteen hundreds. We had done it up when we got married in 1970 giving our accommodation three bedrooms and a bathroom upstairs and a farmhouse kitchen, hall/dinning room and small sitting room downstairs.

We duly set about furnishing our spare bedroom to an acceptable standard for bed and breakfast; we bought a black oak bedroom suite from a house in Chester after seeing it advertised in the local paper. As Rhyl was, in those days, a popular sea side town. There was a wonderful company called Twiltex which sold all sorts of bedding and soft furnishings suitable for accommodation providers. I made a number of visits over the years to this establishment. Bunk beds for the small bedroom for our girls to sleep in came from there. My husband, being a good handyman, painted a B&B sign and we asked the residents who lived across the road from the Holy Well if we could put it in their garden. It sits there to this day although the people who bought the farm from us when we retired no longer run it as a Bed and Breakfast. We also had another sign at the bottom of the road to direct people up to the farm.

CHAPTER 2
WE WERE IN BUSINESS

It was that simple.

A knock came on our door, our first customers. A pleasant young couple who had seen the sign at the Holy Well wanted to stay for one night. All went well. There was a pub, The Royal Oak, at the end of the road so they walked down for dinner and I only had to provide them with a good farmhouse breakfast. How difficult could it be? My nerves where a jangle as it was my first time but they seemed happy with everything I had provided. They paid me and left and I changed the bedding in anticipation of more customers.

Not difficult at all. Easy cash in my pocket for a few hours work.

THAT'S HOW MY 35 YEAR CAREER IN CATERING STARTED.

NOW FOR THE MANY 'EXPERIENCES' WE HAD PROVIDING ACCOMMODATION.

The second knock on the door proved to be more difficult. There were two couples, travelling together in one car. They were Americans who had visited the Well and wanted to stay the night. I liked the idea of making double money but what to do? The only thing I could do was to let one couple have our bedroom and put us in the children's room. I explained what I had to do and they were quite happy. While they walked down to the Royal Oak for dinner I busily changed the bedding in our room and tidied everything away to make it presentable. I sorted out all sorts of spare bedding so that we could sleep on the floor in the children's room. We didn't have sleeping bags just an assortment of blankets and pillows.

THAT WAS THE FIRST AND LAST TIME WE EVER EVER SLEPT ON THE FLOOR.

We didn't want to disturb the children so, after changing in the bathroom; we had to creep into the bedroom. Making sure there were no guests on the landing before we crossed. It was already a hot summer evening and even hotter with four of us in such a small room, it was very uncomfortable. We tried to keep as quiet as mice but we couldn't sleep a wink. First we needed to get up and open the window, very quietly. Then we needed the bathroom again. Very quietly we opened the bedroom door and peeped through to make sure there was no one on the landing before creeping to the bathroom. We vowed there and then never to do that again. If you are working you need your sleep. We rose the next morning in a sorry state having had very little sleep so with the money made from the booking off we went back to Twiltex to buy a pair of single beds and bedding. The children's bunk beds went into our bedroom, the singles into the smaller room and I bought more furniture in Stan Brown's sale room in Holywell. We became experts at furniture moving, it almost became the norm over the years as ideas changed. I also became a familiar figure in Stan's sale room over the next few years and even in our retirement we still have a number of our buys from there. After one of our improvement jobs across the house I had guests booked but not enough dinning tables and chairs for them. There was a drop leaf priory table and six matching chairs in Stan Browns and my husband, who was harvesting at the time, sent me to the saleroom with the words 'Don't come back without them'. I had had plenty of 'auction' experience as my father was a sheep dealer. Back in the day I had even watched him 'ringing'. This is when a number of buyers get together and toss up who is going to buy the sheep so that they didn't run each other up and they can keep the price low, this is now illegal. I often bought confidently in the sale room but today was different; I didn't like being forced to keep bidding past, what I thought was the right price. There was another gentleman in the sale room who also wanted the table and chairs and we just kept bidding against each other for the table which was first to be sold. My nerves where on edge as I kept having to put up my hand to bid, time after time. I knew I'd paid a lot for it but I had no option. The other gentleman was so mad that I'd outbid him he ran me up on the chairs as well. At that time they seemed a very expensive set but twenty five years later they had earned me back every penny.

As we shared a sitting room with the guests getting to bed early was almost impossibility. It was lovely talking to people from all over the world and they loved to ask all about the farm and the area and what to visit and what not to visit. The downside was trying to escape from them as we had an early start but they were on holiday and in no rush to go to bed. My husband was up at 5am to deliver milk to two hundred customers before milking the cows. I would have to fetch the cows in and put things ready for his return before going back to the house to feed and dress two children and then feed our guests.

On one memorable occasion a lady had booked her parents in for the weekend to celebrate their Golden Wedding anniversary. They were a lovely couple and on their return from dinner in the Royal Oak they asked us to join them for a celebratory drink. We were often asked to join people for a drink but this was different. The couple in question where Polish and they explained that when they opened a bottle of Whisky they drank until it was empty. It was lucky that this was only a half bottle of whisky but with a very small bottle of Canada Dry. We have never been big drinkers and I twigged early into the evening what was going on and made my whisky last. My husband didn't and, cut a long story short; I pushed him up the stairs in a sorry state. He can't remember how many cows he milked the next morning as he was seeing double.

Later on we caught on to the then popular hobby of home brewing and would share many a glass of home-made wine with our guests who, themselves would struggle up the stairs! We would often offer guests a glass of home brew with their evening meal, free of course, as we didn't have a drinks license. After our early experiences sharing a sitting room we decided not to apply for a drinks license as we would then have to stay up to serve guests and because we both had early starts in a morning it wasn't a feasible proposition.

We went to a home brew club in Prestatyn with an elderly gentleman called Herbert Hall who taught us all we know about making wine from fruits and cereals. He was the original eco warrior; he even ran his heating boiler on junk mail which came through the post until he nearly set the house on fire! We also got to know a lovely lady called May Parry who had an MBE for her work as a nurse in Egypt during the war, she told us stories of going back to Cairo for a reunion and getting into a Cairo taxi. The driver told her the only thing he checked every morning was his horn and his brakes. As long as they worked he could get through the Cairo traffic as there were no rules on those roads. This kind lady gave Clare a picture of a shepherdess with her lambs painted by a famous French artist as a Christening gift.

We soon learnt how to make some very strong wine, up to 15% proof. If you then added a pint of spirit to a gallon of wine you ended up, another year later, with a beautiful liqueur. Some friend were none too keen on trying our home brew so we used to make a party punch bowl of two bottle of white home brew, two of red home brew, whisky, ginger ale and lemonade. It was very drinkable with a terrible kick. One of our neighbours, Tony, drank it like pop one night. He wasn't so good the next day. We had got our own back for the night he'd given my husband home-made beer on top of wine with dinner. That had madc him so ill I'd had to milk. He couldn't even find the cows never mind count double numbers. He sat on an upturned bucket at the back of the milking parlour whispering instructions.

We had a black poplar tree in the children's play area onto which we built a stand with pallets and put up a huge rope swing which kept children happy for hours but as with all things, it got old and one very windy day we went out and came home to find the tree had fallen down and almost taken an apple tree with it. As it had given us so much pleasure over the years we decided to give it a good send off with a bonfire party. The previous year we had had a lot of damsons from my old home in Cheshire and made 5 gallons of damson wine and so we saved one demijohn and added a pint of brandy. It was with this liqueur that we toasted our favourite tree with all our friends on a cold crisp November 5th. Black poplar trees are quite rare and were usually planted for special occasions but we really never found out why ours had been planted. The swing was replaced with a bought swing; it was never quite the same.

In the 1970's our accommodation was basic. Shared bathrooms, no tea or coffee facilities, few luxuries and we needed to know how we compared to others. After we had put the B&B sign up we decided to book a farm B&B ourselves so be bought a book of accommodations called 'Stay on a Farm' from WH Smiths and booked a family room on a farm just over the Scottish border near Annan. When we got there I knocked on the front door. Through the window I could see a couple sat on a bench in a very bare room with just a bench and a table and a stone floor. A young lady came to the door and told us that the farmer had put them in there an hour before and they were waiting for his wife. I didn't like the looks of it at all; it was so cold, dark and bare looking and so we drove back to the local petrol station and asked there, explaining our predicament. The petrol attendant told us that in the B&B we had booked they would put people who didn't even know each other in the same room if they could fit them in but he recommended another lady, Mrs. Hogg. They had a pig and corn farm further along the same road. Yes the Hogg's had hogs and plenty of them, over 200 if I remember rightly all fed on the corn that they grew themselves. We arrived at the Hogg's to find she had a family room available which was lovely; the whole place was clean and homely, just what we wanted. We stayed two nights and on the second night she made us an evening meal and baby sat the children so we could go to the pub for a drink. This was an example we would model ourselves on.

CHAPTER 3
THE STAY ON A FARM BOOK.

Our first paid advert was in the Stay on a Farm book. We had visited various book shops to see what people bought and found that all the shops stocked this book as it was so popular. From this and our own experience we realised that families expected an evening meal to be available especially if they wanted to stay for the week. I'm a good basic cook so farmhouse meals were no problem. My mother had Rheumatoid Arthritis so, as the oldest daughter, I had taken over many of her jobs which included the cooking. I cooked my first full family Christmas Dinner when I was 18 years old. Mum was one of six children which had led to fifteen grandchildren for her parents. Every Christmas we would have a family party, when I was younger this would be in Granny and Granddads but as they got older their children would take it in turns to host the party. I distinctly remember sitting thirty people around two tables in our old farmhouse kitchen. At that time we had an old fashioned fire grate with oven next to it and the turkey was so big we had to keep the door shut with a piece of wood propped up against it. Each family fetched cutlery with coloured thread on the handles so that we knew whose was whose and they would also bring a sweet. Catering for big numbers was something I was brought up with.

Our first one week booking for Bed Breakfast and Evening Meal was for a family of three, Mum, Dad and their small son who was about six or seven years old. By this time we had put a set of bunk beds in the double bedroom. We ended up with bunk beds everywhere, three or four sets at one time. I sat down to plan a week's menu of three course dinners. I planned cold starters and hot sweets or visa versa and roast dinners to cold salads, a general mix of good farmhouse meals, there were no choices on the menu at that time, just the three courses. I planned my shopping list and prepared some courses in advance to freeze to save work. I thought I'd prepared for everything. I was tense, this was a first for me and I still had our two young children to look after. The family arrived on the Saturday and all was going well, I did try to get an afternoon nap on the Monday with one daughter in school and the other still having a couple of hours sleep in the afternoon. Well that didn't work as the family came back early and disturbed me, I felt I had to be on hand in case they wanted something.

That first full week was exhausting, mainly because I was so on edge. The one thing I hadn't prepared for was the toilet paper. This family, I'm convinced, ate toilet paper; in fact they used a roll a day. I was brought up right in the middle of the countryside in Cheshire, five miles from a shop and my mother didn't drive so we only shopped once a week when Dad took us into town. If you ran out of something you did without it. The more often you shop the more you buy. Not that week, I couldn't manage without toilet paper now could I although I did have memories of my father's mother cutting up newspaper to use as toilet paper but I didn't think that would have been appropriate. So back up to town I had to go to stock up on toilet paper. I was appalled by this over usage of toilet paper; it was something which annoyed me for years. I still can't believe how much toilet paper some people use. Over the years I've tried cheap paper and better paper and I did find that guests used less of the Andrex and more of the cheap brands so that is what I bought. When I went to the wholesalers I would buy big catering size packs of toilet paper which held about eighteen packs of two rolls, in whatever colour I fancied on the day. Once I bought peach coloured paper. We had two American boys staying and they couldn't get over the colour, so taken where they that they bought some rolls to take home to put in their bathroom when they had a party. To this day I really don't know if you can or can't buy peach coloured toilet paper in America.

The 'Stay on a Farm' book kept me busy with customers through the summer holidays and the two weeks of Easter. I never took people over Christmas, firstly we had so much more work on the farm in the winter with all the cattle inside and secondly we wanted to enjoy Christmas with our children. The rest of the time things where quieter, just the odd weekend guest or overseas visitors touring the UK. For the six weeks of the summer holidays I could be cooking for up to fourteen people per day, including us. Things could get busy and I needed some help so John asked one of our milk customers if her daughter wanted a summer holiday job and this is how Claire came to join the crew. She was such fun to work with. She would walk down from Holywell, enter the house and kick her off shoes. She would then set tables, and help out with anything I needed before putting her shoes

back on again to wait on tables at meal time. We had some good times together.
She was always ready with her humorous opinion of some of our guests. Most of our guests where families who came for a weeks holiday in the country, near the sea side. This was before the advent of cheap air fares to the sun. This meant that the children played with our children and so the kitchen was often full of children and sometimes adults, even when I was trying to cook meals. It was a bit like Piccadilly Circus with everyone coming and going. I could never get my two children to bed as the other children where on holiday and allowed to stay up late, then I couldn't get our two up in a morning but most of the time they had great fun together even going out with guests for the day. Just occasionally there would be children who ours didn't want to play with and they would hide to avoid mixing with them. Even if some children didn't speak English they would play together, rain or shine.

One of my earliest memories from this time was then we had a family with three children staying along with a couple from Elgin in Scotland with their only son who had his arm in plaster. He had broken his arm the week before their holiday. This was a blessing in disguise and his boy was so full of mischief. He was into everything, so much so that one day he fell from the bales in the hay shed and his parents had to take him up to the local Cottage Hospital to make sure he hadn't damaged his arm again. Luckily he hadn't. Our daughters had a trials motor cycle at that time and many an evening was spent in the fields with my husband in charge of teaching these children how to ride a motor cycle. Whether this was a good thing or not we never learnt!

During one week of the summer holidays we had the King family, the parents were a teacher and a university professor. I don't know when we had such badly behaved children. It was a wet week and they kept running in and out without wiping their feet, they would then run upstairs and jump on the beds with dirty shoes. They jumped so hard they put the bed leg through the floor. This bedroom overlooked the farmyard and was later our bedroom. At that time, before we had altered the far end of the house, we slept in the back-middle room which lead out onto the landing which hadn't been improved. When we had renovated the far end of the house we moved yet again to the back room overlooking the yard so that we could hear the cattle outside at night. It's necessary to hear the cows, especially if one is due to calve. They make a different noise in labour to their day to day moo. When we moved into this room we had to have the floor properly repaired where the bed leg had gone through the floor. We also had fitted wardrobes and cupboards built by our local joiner, Keith. This was so that we could straighten out the wonky walls. I did have to ask the parents to control their children's behaviour but the parents just ignored them and let them run riot. I'm sure some people were of the opinion that if they were on holidaying that the break included a holiday from being responsible for their children. I eventually just treated all children in the same way as I treated my own. I've told off many a child in front of their parents and not been stopped. I even had to stop a young child from sticking his fingers into a three point plug socket in front of his mother. Anyway, after a week of this I told Claire that our next booking was for the Williams family, Granny, Granddad, their daughter and granddaughter. Claire assured me that with a name like Williams they would be normal and peace would reign. No such luck, when she walked through the door and kicked off her shoes I announced to her that the Williams family were Jamaican from London. Well she just fell about laughing. What a week we had with the Jamaicans.

Lovely people, well behaved children but! Granddad had only passed his driving test in London three weeks before they arrived and bought himself a car to bring his family on holiday. They couldn't read a map (it was more of a case of 'what is a map'), and had no ideas about distances, places or the time it took to drive from A to B. Dinner was served at 6.30pm for everyone as I cooked one main meal with, maybe a choice of sweet or starter, well not for the Williams family. On the second day they set off for Snowdon, I did tell them that it was an hours drive away, to get to the railway to the summit, a must on any tourist 'to do' list. It was 8pm before they arrived back, very apologetic as they hadn't realised the time because they had had such a wonderful day out enjoying Snowdon and all it had to offer. On the third night they just went down to Rhyl to the beach. In the 1980's Rhyl was still a thriving sea side resort, the beach would be full of holiday makers sunbathing, swimming and making sand castles. On the seafront you could roller skate and buy cockles and mussels or a Clwyd ice cream. The family had driven back to the farm along the coast road and followed the Hoylake signs instead of the Holywell signs and ended up on the Wirral Peninsular, about 15 miles away. Late for dinner again, 8.30pm this time and again they apologised profusely, such lovely people really. This went on all week, they were never less than thirty minutes late for a meal, I was tearing my hair out as some meals don't keep as well as others, they just spoil sitting in the oven waiting for hours. On the Friday night a part had broken in the milking parlour and so John had to go up to Holywell for a replacement before he could milk the cows. When he came back, just after 5pm, he popped into the house to tell me all would be fine with the Williams as they were parked in the car park in Holywell so I could expect them to be back on time. John is such a car freak he recognises cars and car numbers wherever we are. We could be driving up a motorway and he will say 'I know that car; it's parked in such and such a road'. No such luck, they only went and locked themselves out of their car and had to call out the AA to get into the car, one hour late this time. Every single night that week they came back late for dinner. It meant that every single day I was up at 6.30am and didn't sit down until after 9pm and was then on call until everyone had gone to bed. Claire arrived on the Saturday morning to hear me moaning yet again about the Williams family. When they came to pay they gave me the biggest tip I'd ever had and told me what a wonderful time they had had.

It was so hard to be cross with them, I felt so guilty about all the things I'd said about them all week. On leaving they told me that they wouldn't be taking the motorway home, they would go through the countryside as it would be much more pleasant. I did wonder if they ever made it back to London!

The 'Von Trapp' family where another lovely family, obviously not their real name, just the one we gave them. They were a German family consisting of Mum, Dad and four children but, like the Von Trapp children in the film The Sound of Music, they were regimented. Mum and Dad sat top and bottom of the dinner table with two children on each side. Their manners where immaculate, they were always on time, a pleasure to serve and their rooms where left very tidy. On the Sunday night I gave them trifle as a sweet. I explained to them that this was a traditional 'special occasion' desert in the UK. After they had eaten, the father announced in his usual stern voice that it was like eating your way through a sweet shop. I have always remembered that and think it's such a wonderful description of trifle.

Another memorable child was Tania, O my god, we won't forget that name. Tania came with her American mother. They had booked for four nights with us though a Tourist Board scheme which allowed people to buy a package holiday on farms throughout Wales. The customer paid the Tourist Board and the Tourist Board paid the B&B proprietors. This New York lady had arrived without her husband as he was a high flying business man and couldn't find the time to come on holiday, so she told us. I was also informed that they had been out and bought a whole wardrobe of new clothes suitable for staying on farms. I just thought we all wore similar cloths, I didn't know there was a need for specific 'farm' clothes on holiday other than a pair of wellingtons which they didn't bring. Mother was dressed to the nines in designer clothes and shoes with makeup and nail varnish to match. I really don't know what she did all day as she hardly left her bedroom and Tania was left to her own devices. Our children didn't like her one tiny bit, they spent hours just trying to avoid her. None of the other children staying or their parents liked her, especially when she took to walking into anyone or everyone's rooms. One parents asked me what she should do and I told her, the same as I was doing, tell her off. This wasn't the most memorable thing about this child and her mother. It was when the mother decided she needed Tania for something. She would open her bedroom window and, without even noticing the beautiful view from the back of the house up over the green field dotted with black and white cows, and beyond to Brynford mountain behind she would shout, in that harsh New York accent-- TANIA, TANIA, TANIA. It has put me off the name for the rest of my life. Towards the end of their stay I rang the Tourist Board and asked for the names of the next farms where they had booked to stay on so that I could warn them about what was about to arrive.

CHAPTER 4
OVERSEAS VISITORS

As time went on we did join other organisations like the Welsh Tourist Board and the AA so that we could advertise with them. The Stay on a Farm book did go out of fashion with people and is now out of print. These other adverts brought in more overseas customers especially during the early 1980s. This made for such an interesting mix of people I felt we almost went round the world without even moving from our home.

We did learn a lot about accents and how to identify where people came from. As in the UK accents are often different in the same country. The most difficult UK accent to understand is the Scottish. You really do have to concentrate to pick up exactly what they are saying. And if you get it wrong when guessing if someone is from Yorkshire or Lancashire you are really in trouble they are still very protective of their origins in the North of England after the Wars of the Roses although the wars took place over six hundred years ago in the fourteen hundreds between the House of Plantagenet (the white rose) and the House of Lancaster (the red rose).

We found the New York accent from America especially harsh, but the accents softened further south until you had a real drawl in what they call the Deep South. Australians and Canadians where soon identified but South Africans always fooled me, the accent had an Australian way about it. The one way to identify a South African was the way they left their bedrooms. In South Africa most white families have staff. This mcans they never, ever tidy up after themselves. They just drop everything after they have used it, towels just dropped by the wash basin, dirty underwear at the side of the bed, bedding strewn everywhere. Their bedrooms where a nightmare to work on, it would take ages just picking up towels etc. and folding dropped cloths to get to the beds to even start to make them. But they would always make such a big thing of saying that they didn't know how I managed on my own. I really should have enlightened them to the fact that I would have managed a lot better if they had been tidier but as my rules list on the kitchen wall said,

Rule number 1 'The customer is always right'
Rule number 2 'When the customer is wrong remember rule number one - 'the customer is always right'.

The Scandinavian's were a free-spirited people, walking round with just towels round their waists, not caring who was about. They were really easy-going people and lovely to share our home with. When we were still sharing a bathroom with our guests John went up to the bathroom after breakfast one morning to meet the Swedish husband of the couple staying, on the landing by the bathroom door. After smiling politely at each other John proceeded to open the bathroom door, it wasn't locked, and there stood in front of him in the bathroom was the Swedish wife totally naked without a care in the world. He was so shocked he just stood there for a moment; well that's what he told me. Her husband had made no attempt to warn him that she was in there and she wasn't in the least bit embarrassed by the confrontation. This experience happened early on in our career but such experiences carried on right through to the last weeks we were doing the job. A man called Nigel was staying with us while visiting his children in 2011. He was the son-in-law of one of our neighbours, Malcolm and Jean. Nigel came in late, got up late and wandered around the house with just a towel around him. He had booked his stay without breakfast, bed only as he ate with Malcolm and Jean. Booking without breakfast didn't become the norm until a few years before we retired when they opened a McDonalds just outside Holywell and the younger generation would prefer to go there than to sit at a table.

The French where they only people I really couldn't get on with. They thought they knew it all, not just one particular family but the French in general. The only French family I can say I liked stayed just after the Falkland's wars. The husband worked for the company who made the Exocet missiles and he felt so bad about them being used to attack the British during the war. That family had lived in America for a number of years and so understood how our minds worked. One particularly difficult French family consisted of Mum, Dad and two teenage sons. They would lounge in the sitting room with their feet up on the coffee table and stop other guests from using the room by their rude behaviour. One day when I went up to clean their bedroom they had rinsed out four pairs of denim jeans and pegged them to the curtain rail. They were dripping onto the floor! At that time I did have a utility room which the guests could use to dry clothes but they could have hung their clothes out on my washing line if they had only asked.

Another French couple were given a back bedroom but, at milking time they came down to demand another room as they couldn't possibly put up with the noise of the milking machine for an hour, they came from the countryside you know. May be they still milked by hand in France but an hour twice a day to listen to a dull hum wasn't asking much. It was the one and only time anyone complained about the milking machine noise. They should have expected some machinery noise on a farm especially as 'they came from the countryside you know'.

We did have a difficult Spanish family to deal with but it wasn't entirely their fault. There suitcases had got left in Spain by Ryanair Air which meant that every night they had to wash their clothes as they had no clean ones to change into. This meant that the washing machine and dryer where on until all hours. They also kept the children up late and the Spanish children would run around the landing late into the night keeping everyone else awake. On the third night the eight-year-old managed to wet the bed which left me with a big job in the morning washing it and drying it out with an electric fan heater. Spare mattresses where not something I kept in stock.

We had a number of German guests over the years and the older generation of guest were always very apologetic about the War. As I wasn't old enough to remember the war I would accept their apologies with good grace and carry on. Many German guests felt they had to apologise for the War, especially those who had lived through it as children. I do remember one gentleman telling me how he and his friends would follow the American soldiers around for anything they could get out of them to either eat or to sell, as they were so hungry.

Most Germans spoke good English and one afternoon I was talking to a German girl while setting the dining room tables. Our daughter Clare came in and I asked her to fetch me something. I turned to the lady and told her that Clare was my Gofor. She asked me what a Gofor was, she said she had never heard that word before and so I had to explain that a Gofor goes for this and goes for that, it was shortened version of 'Go for this or Go for that'. We do have a wonderful language don't we? She went away pleased to have learnt a new English word.

Two years after the Berlin Wall had fallen we had our first East European's; they were teachers from East Germany. They told us that they had not been allowed to learn English under the communist government but they had taught themselves the language in two years. Their English would put you to shame, it was so good. I had no trouble at all understanding them. That was the opposite of two Spanish boys who stayed once who understood no English at all. When they came to pay me they just handed me a wad of money. I took the correct amount and returned the rest to them. I did wonder how often they had been ripped off during their visit to the UK.

Three nurses from Malaysia just giggled through the whole of their stay with us. They were lovely girls who worked as nurses in London but they had no car, they had come by train to Flint and come by taxi up to the farm for a weekend away. On the Sunday we said we would take them to Snowdon so we packed a picnic hamper and set off with the three nurses, Susan and Jennifer. They did so enjoy their visit and we enjoyed having them and giving them an experience they otherwise wouldn't have had.

An Irish lady had booked in her three Irish sons for a short stay with us and when they arrived they fetched me a gift, of a two-foot-long shilalie (An Irish shillaly is a walking stick). They said that Customs had taken them to one side and questioned them about it, what were they going to use it for etc? They had explained that it was a gift and then they were allowed into the country with it. After they had left I went to clean their room and they had only gone and left their passports in the dressing table draw. Luckily I was able to contact the mother from the address on the booking letter and she was able to contact them at their next farm stay. Things were different in the days before mobile phones, trying to contact people who where en route could be a nightmare in an emergency.

Now and then someone would leave something in the room and, at first I would try and contact them but, in the long run I found it easier if I waited for them to contact me, I didn't always have a phone number or a full address to send things to. If a child had left their teddy bear the family came back that day as no sleep could be had without it.

I've had to post all sorts of things back to people who left treasured goods and have a number of appreciative thank you letters. A German lady left a beautiful silver topped tartan umbrella which I hoped wouldn't be claimed as I really liked it but she rang me and asked me to post it back to Germany and she would pay the postage. Have you ever tried to parcel up an umbrella? - Not easy! I gave its some serious thought and came up with a cunning plan. I went down to Abakan, a local shop which sells material, and begged the centre cardboard roll off a roll of material. This covered the long length of the umbrella. I then covered the handle with the centre cardboard of a toilet roll and taped them together. When this was done I covered it all in brown paper and labelled it. Off I went to the Post Office and queued up with all the nice square parcels to weigh and pay for my 'machine gun' - well that's what it looked like. It did eventually find its way home and a nice thank you letter came with the money to cover postage as promised.

Heather Johnson left her evening bag and sent us a short thank you note with postage stamps to cove the cost or returning it. Jill Watts managed to leave her necklace behind and sent the stamps for postage and added 'thanks again for looking after us so well at the weekend. It was lovely to meet you and your husband'. Sue Grinnell managed to leave some cloths behind! Another parcel had to be sent with a Just a Note card in return to thank us.

Returning things worked the other way around as well. Sometimes guests would take their room key with them and so I put big plastic tags on them with our address write on them. The keys would then appear back through the post, some with just a stamp added to the plastic tag and some in envelopes of various sizes. For some strange reason the key for bedroom number three would go walk about the most often. This was just a double room and not a family room were a harassed mum or dad would just forget to give it to me so I never did understand why this key liked to travel. I letter from Hiroshi Sakura came which came back with number three key in April 1998 saying, and I quote: 'I just want to say sorry about the key, and how much we enjoyed the stay in your farmhouse.'

We quite often had Irish guests who, during The Troubles, told us how relaxed they would feel in the UK compared with home, especially those from Northern Ireland. We had a Church of Ireland minister, his wife and three children staying for four nights during The Troubles. I had no other guests staying at the time but the Minister insisted on talking about the Catholics in a whisper as if he was afraid of what he said in case the wrong person heard him. It must have been difficult to live in those conditions, never knowing if a bomb would explode. I local lady I know was brought up in Northern Island and the children were taught in school to get down and hide if they heard an explosion. She told me that her father was taking her and her sister to school one day and they had stopped at the petrol station for fuel. I bomb went off close by and both girls shot down into the foot well of the car. She said their father told them how well they had been taught. A local dignitary had been bombed in the garage forecourt. She told me in such a matter of fact manner, as if it was just part of their normal lives, which I suppose it was at that time.

On two occasions I wasn't too happy with the reasons that Irish where staying with me. Maybe in retrospect it was because many of them felt they had to be careful about what they said to strangers. Anyway, on these two occasions I rang the local police and raised my concerns giving them the guest's names and car registration numbers. On both occasions the police rang me back and told me they had checked out the details and that the people where not suspects of any sort. I apologised to the police but they said they would rather I rang and all was well than that I didn't ring.

Over the years we had two opera singers who stayed and needed to practise for shows when they returned home. They would walk up the fields so as not to disturb us and so we would just stand outside and listen to them. One gentleman was Australian and the other Canadian.

Our youngest daughter, Clare, was born in 1986, a point where we were well into the business of providing for guests. After she was born I did very few evening meals as I was trying to reduce my work load with a baby to look after as well. She was brought up with strangers in the house and thought nothing of it. On one occasion, she would only be about 3 years old, she took a young Chinese boy up to her sister's bedroom and they played with Jennifer's makeup. Jennifer was not too happy but not half as upset as the Chinese parents who couldn't believe that a boy would dream of putting makeup all over his face. Boys are revered in China; they didn't want a boy who acted like a girl. The pair of them looked a pretty sight with lipstick everywhere even in their hair.

At that time the Australians got a long 6-8 weeks holiday if they have worked for a company for over fifteen years. This was because so many of them where from overseas and would want to visit family at a time before the long-haul flights were as good as they are today. Often they would be over for a few weeks seeing Europe and UK. In Britain they would hire a car and travel around the country. My utility room was next to the guest's sitting room and they had access to it and so I gave the guests the use of the facilities and put the machines onto a pay meter. I had many a guest who just came for the washing machine. If you are away from home for a long time you don't want to spend 'holiday' time finding a laundrette and washing cloths and so they would put their washing in my machine in a morning and I would sort it for them. Or at night before they went out for dinner in would go a load of washing. Many a guest was very grateful for my washer and drier. One Australian couple while staying with us, looked through our Guest book and found that his boss had stayed with us two weeks before he had. He was looking forward to telling the boss when he got home.

Australian children, staying on a farm had to be taught that nettles sting. Apparently, there are no nettle plants in Australia and children would treat nettle plants in the same way as any other plant not realising what happens when you touch them. Nettles were probably easier to deal with than some of the Australian creatures such as snakes or big spiders, we each get used to our own local problems don't we.

A New Zealand couple who stayed told us that they had had some American friends for many years and that when they last visited them they took a stone fish from their garden. They now sent letters from wherever they visited with a picture of the fish in it and a letter letting what a wonderful time the fish was having. I was asked if I could stand outside my front door holding the small stone fish and looking puzzled. I had my picture taken so many times outside my front door but this one beat the others standing.

Sometimes you just had to support guests who had a problem, and this happened with the family of a rather highly strung German undertaker. They were on their way back to our house driving east along the A55 on a Sunday evening. There was a very bad accident on the other side of the road which slowed down all the traffic on their side because people were looking to see what had happened. This resulted in a bumper to bumper crash in which they were involved, and which wrote off their car. They rang me at about 7.30pm in a flap, not knowing what to do. Their English was very poor and so I had to go to Abergele police station to collect them and then take them to Glan Clwyd hospital as their son had injured his arm in the crash. We waited in the accident department until the arm could be x-rayed and, luckily, it was not broken, just bruised. The police had asked us to go back to the police station so that the family could give them a statement of what had happened. They spoke so little English but the police wanted a statement in English which was going to be impossible. The police tried to call in an interpreter and so we sat there waiting. The poor husband was getting very agitated by it all, walking up and down, wringing his hands, and chain smoking. The policeman kept coming in and out of the interview room telling us they were having trouble on a Sunday trying to get an interpreter and that the police in the headquarters in Llandudno where insisting on an English statement. Everyone was getting edgy by now; it was late at night and the children were tired, so in the end they decided that we could all go back to my B&B and report to Holywell police station at 10am on the Monday morning where an interpreter would be sent for the statement to be given. I fed all my guests the next morning and took the German family up to Holywell Police station. They knew nothing about what had gone on and there was no interpreter. In fact they hadn't been told we were to be there. They were much more understanding of the situation and so they just asked the husband and wife to write a statement of what had happened in German. They said that they would then send the statements back to Abegele and they could get them interpreted. What a performance, we could all have had an easier time if they had done that the night before. A new hire car was sorted with much less fuss so that the family could carry on with their holiday.

In the 1980's with traffic getting busier the town of Holywell decided it needed a ring road to ease the congestion in the High Street. It was to run to the north of the town through some old buildings which had to be demolished before work could start. It all caused some difficulties while it was being built both for road uses and shower users, yes shower users. When the old properties where demolished lots of old water pipers where uprooted. Unbeknown to me, this had the effect of blocking every shower in Holywell with grit blocking up the shower heads. Now the Americans love their showers, a bath just won't do at all. An American gentleman came down one evening ringing the bell for attention to complain that his shower wouldn't work. I went up and looked at it and, not knowing what to do to repair it, I gave him another, larger room with a shower; the other rooms had baths in them. Half an hour later he was down again, this shower wouldn't work either. By now he was furious and gave me a real mouthful raising his voice for everyone to hear. I apologised profusely but, as I didn't know what the problem was and I couldn't get a plumber out at that time of night, there was nothing I could do. The next morning he was no happier and paid me and left. I managed to get the plumber to visit that day, explaining what had gone on. He was the one that told me what had caused the problem; he had spent days going around the town unblocking shower heads. That evening an Australian guest, who had overhead the confrontation the night before, rang the bell and presented me with a bunch of flowers because had had been so disgusted at the behaviour of the American man. It restored my faith in human nature. This event happened at a bad time for me as, the previous day I had come out of hospital after suffering a miscarriage. I would have been in 1985 as I had two miscarriages the year before Clare was born. I didn't tell the guests what had happened as my troubles were not important to them; they wanted to have trouble free holidays and it was my job to aide that in every way I could.

I was inspected regularly by both the AA and the Welsh Tourist Board and did various tourism courses over the years, organised by the Welsh Tourist Board. I was also inspected by the local councils Health and Hygiene department. Most of these resulted in a certificate which I would put up where the guests could see them. A French gentleman was most taken with my 'Cordon Bleu' certificate although I didn't have a cookery certificate on show he had seen my 'Basic Food Hygiene Certificate'. When he came down to breakfast he asked me to make him scrambled eggs on toast and handed me a full garlic, not just a clove, which he asked to be crushed and added to the eggs. It stunk the house out. I've been asked for various strange dietary requests over the years, but I think that was the most memorable. It's quite amazing to hear what foods some people are allergic to.

One year we had a gentleman from Patagonia staying. A large number of Welsh people had emigrated to Patagonia over 150 years ago and they had stayed and formed their own Welsh speaking community. This gentleman was rather disappointed that neither John nor I spoke Welsh. John does understand some Welsh. His father was Welsh but his mother was a Lancashire lass who had come over to Wales as a land girl during the war. I was born in Wales and learnt Welsh when I first went to school in Wrexham but when my grandfather died we returned to the family farm in Cheshire and consequently only spoke English. I was only 7 years old when we moved back to Cheshire and have forgotten any of the Welsh I learnt in school although I must admit to knowing a few of the swear words that my father in law used. We did manage to find a Male Voice Choir who let people listen to their practise nights. The Patagonian gentleman went to this and by talking to the singers, found out about a pub where Welsh singing took place on a Saturday night. This was not someone who would perform in the pub; it was the locals who would have a sing along after a few beers. This was a common thing throughout Wales.

A story which was closer to home involved John's nearest neighbours down the lane, Mr. and Mrs. Bailey and their two children both of whom where older than John. He remembers as a small child buying toffee apples off them which they sold through a window which was directly onto the road. In those days there were more houses and children in Bryn Celyn than there are today with two rows of 18 terraced houses. Mrs. Bailey became ill and eventually became an invalid. The children were still young and so they employed a young lady to live in and look after the children and the house. Eventually Mrs. Bailey died and the two children married and left home. Mr. Bailey then married the housekeeper. It was at about this time that John and I were married and set up the Bed and Breakfast. Mr. Bailey had died in the early 1970's leaving the second Mrs. Bailey on her own. One day Mrs. Bailey, who must have been in her late 60's now, came up in great excitement to book a Canadian lady in to stay with us. She told me that she had been brought up by nuns in a Liverpool children's home and had no idea of what or who her family were. She found out that her mother had died in Canada. The step sisters where sorting out their mother's belongings and found out that a child had been left in England. They had managed to trace her and one of them was visiting. It was when the step sister had arrived that she found out the full story which had been preserved in her mother's records. Mrs. Baileys father had died when she was just a child and her mother wanted to remarry but the second husband didn't want the child from her first husband and so the young child was put into the children's home before they left for a new life in Canada where two more girls where born. They had a wonderful time together and Mrs. Bailey was invited over to Canada. This was her first and only time abroad and she was so excited. On her return she came up to tell us all about it. She was a small, frail looking lady and she'd been quite surprised when the airline people took her under their wing and found her a wheel chair, sorted her luggage and put her on the plane first. They had treated her like royalty and she had had a wonderful experience with her new-found Canadian family. Sadly Mrs. Bailey died a few years later but she died a much happier lady for finding her family after so many years.

CHAPTER 5
THE AMERICANS.

When Clare was 12 years old and playing a saxophone in the school band, we had two members of the Denver, Colorado concert orchestra staying one of whom was a bass saxophone player. They, with the rest of the concert band, were playing in a concert in Chester, on their UK tour. This couple had decided not to travel on the band bus but to hire a car and stay in the countryside, rather than in the various cities they were performing in. When they found out that Clare played a tenor saxophone the husband showed her his bass saxophone and asked her if she wanted to watch the concert. I thought she may be shy on her own so suggested they took her and her friend. Off they went for an evening out. The girls were given front row seats in the hall in the Queens School, Chester, and after the show they were introduced to the band. The girls were also invited to their hotel to join them for dinner. It was almost midnight when they all got home, we where getting a bit worried as to where they all were especially as the girls had school the next day. When I asked they what the best bit of the whole evening was, thinking what a wonderful experience they must have had, I couldn't have guessed what their answer would be. 'We went around the roundabout five times' was their answer. There are no roundabouts in America; the Americans don't know how to handle them and so, as you may have seen in the American Lampoon family film where the family holiday in the UK, they often just drive round and round to find their way off. This was the greatest moment of their cultural night out!

The Americans would always leave their curtain closed. Up I would go to the bedroom to change the beds only to find these closed curtains, why were they not opening them to look across the Wirral or up across the fields on a beautiful summer morning? It was something I really couldn't understand until we went to the United States in 1992 with the Simmental Cattle Society. We had a pedigree Simmental bull and four pedigree cows, (these are the cattle with the bells round their necks in Switzerland.) On our free day we hired a car and drove out to visit some bed and breakfast guests whose grandparents had emigrated from Holywell and had visited to try and trace any distant family left in the area. I asked Fran why the curtains where drawn and she told me that no one opened their curtains as they needed to keep the heat out.

I also noticed that they have smaller windows than we do for the same reason, along with blinds as well as curtains. I then forgave all Americans for leaving the curtains drawn and not enjoying our views as I understood fully why they did it. As a red-head myself I am not a sun lover, I can burn looking through the window never mind going out in the sun.

One warm summer evening two American gentlemen where taking a walk around the farm building. John had found that a cow was trying to calve but having difficulties. He had brought her down from the field and we were having trouble trying to get her into an appropriate shed to assist her. She was running back and to, not really wanting to go into any shed and getting herself in a stressed state, so we asked the men to help us by standing at the top of the yard near to were we scrapped the muck over into the spreader ready to take out to the field. We asked them to make sure she didn't pass them by waving their arms in the air. This cow knew that they where ignorant of the ways of cows and headed straight for them. Did they wave their arms in the air? No they did not, they ran away from the cow. She promptly jumped over the ramp into the muck spreader. What a do we had, we hitched the tractor onto the spreader and John was driving around the yard with a cow stood up in the back of a spreader which was half full of muck. The men hurried back to the house and left us to sort it all out ourselves. The vet was called, and we proceeded to try and fill the spreader with straw to raise her up to a point where we could roll her out of the spreader onto yet more straw. With the vet's assistance, we managed to calve the cow but she had been in labour too long and the poor calf was born dead.

On another occasion two American gentlemen arrived at the door looking for a night's accommodation. I duly showed them to a twin-bedded room which they were pleased with. These gentlemen looked as most Americans do, casually dressed in denim jeans and tee shirts. Nothing to write home about, just run of the mill Americans. At about 7pm in the evening they rang the bell and asked me if I could provide them with bread and wine. I looked at them in, what must have been, a bewildered fashion and they went on to explain that they were monks and that they wanted to give themselves Holy Communion. In the United States their order didn't wear a uniform. I also had some American nuns who taught in schools who were also casually dressed.

Four Americans booked in for one night and arrived at 2pm in the afternoon. They proceeded to ask me which attraction it was best to see before dinner, Chester or North Wales. Many Americans travelled with a book entitled ‘See Britain in 21days. And many Americans struggled with our narrow lanes and how much longer it took to drive than on their ‘freeways’. The Horseshoe Pass above Llangollen was a road which could put the fear of God into an American driver as on onc sidc you looked up at the mountain and on the other there was a sheer drop to the valley below. I clearly remember one lady whose husband had been driving, telling me she closed her eyes as she couldn’t look at the drop. It was marginally better than our road which was unmade, single track with no passing places and a short drop into a house. I’m certain that some guests just never made it up the road and turned around to find somewhere else to stay. Often American guest would arrive shaking from the experience.

We had a southern US police woman staying one day who had to pull up on the hard shoulder of the motor way to rest and the British police had pulled over to see if her car had broken down. She was a large lady and she had hired a small car for one person, a mini. Her feet where so wide that she had trouble driving a 'shift gear' car. In America most cars are automatics. Her foot crossed onto two pedals at the same time. She said she'd had a lovely talk to the police who had asked her to move on. We asked her if she was armed in the states and she told us that she 'harboured a colt 45.'

Al and Fran from Texas stayed with us over many years. Al's ancestor had been the vicar for the parish of Whitford a couple of miles from Holywell and had emmigrated to the States. When he left the parishioners had had a collection and bought him an organ to take with him. Al and Fran were back to find any long-lost family. They did find a second cousin who was in poor health and not able to visit the States which disappointed Al. They always visited out of season, often into October and Al loved to watch the political party conferences on the TV in an afternoon while Fran took a nap. Al was a 'big' man but all he ever wore were what we would call, baby grows. He had two, one to wash and one to wear. They became friends of some local business people who invited them to dinner, off he went in his 'baby grow' to find that they had made an occasion of it and where dressed in dinner jackets. It didn't bother Al, nothing bothered Al. During one stay Al was watching the political conferences during the afternoon and I was working in the kitchen when 'the earth moved' yes we had a small earthquake, Al came through and asked if that is what it was as he'd never experienced one before. He was quite excited and wanted to know if we had them often. I told him that a few years before we had an even bigger quake in North Wales in the early 1980's when one morning about 8am as I was down stairs sitting drinking a cup of tea at the kitchen table the table moved up and down. I thought either Sue or Jen were banging down the stairs, but it was actually books falling off the shelf in their bedroom. It was a most odd feeling. It did cause the plaster to crack between the different 'builds' in the house, they must each have moved in different ways. When John got back from the milk round he said he hadn't felt a thing but lots of people had rung into the local radio station to say they had felt it. Al was famous for carrying his camcorder on his shoulder wherever he went I really got rather tired of being 'recorded especially when, one day he walked into the kitchen when my hairdresser was washing my hair. It rather put me off having my picture taken. We cursed at the time but a few years on from his first stay he spent one winter putting his films onto the TV in Texas and re-filming bits of our family. We can now watch Clare growing up, old pictures of the garden, the Simmental cattle and even the old Chester Cattle Market. Al was an old-fashioned sort of man and poor Fran had to do as she was told. On two occasions he fetched with him first his daughter and then his son. One day the son had obviously had just too much of his Dad. They had been on a train journey and on the way home Jeff had sat in a different carriage to Mum and Dad. He fell asleep and missed the stop at Flint station. He had to get off at Prestatyn and get a taxi back. His Dad didn't half give him what for. Al had served in the American Army during the Second World Was and had been stationed on the Sandringham estate. He told us that when rations where short someone would go out and shoot a deer on the estate to supplement the food. He said that the King always knew what had happened and a complaint and a 'don't do it again' message would be sent from Sandringham house.

In 1993 we travelled with the Simmental Cattle Society to Dallas, Texas for the Simmental World Congress to co-inside with the Texas state fair. On our day off we hired a car and drove out to see Al and Fran, Al had been diagnosed with lung cancer by now and so, instead of taking him a bottle of Scotch Whisky I took him a box of Kellogg's Bran Flakes, his favourite when he stayed with us but not available in the States. I had a scary moment going through customs. We had to declare that we were going to an Agricultural Show and so we were directed to a different check point. The people in front of us had their suitcases inspected inside and out. Not a pleasant thing for anyone to have done to them in front of everyone by stern looking armed officers. Cloths and shoes were pulled from their suit case and comments such as 'these shoes are too small for you, who are they for' they were gift for the grandchildren. Herbs and seeds were taken from them and confiscated. This made us even more nervous. We didn't admit to anything and, luckily, didn't get searched. When hiring the car for our visit to Al and Fran's we asked for a 'small' car and they gave us a Buick sports car. Well John enjoyed driving this didn't he, especially after we got off the five lane Dallas highway, into the countryside, after trying to remember which side of the road to drive on. He 'enjoyed' it so much that we came over the brow of a hill to be caught by a policeman for speeding. We 'crawled' and showed him our British passports and told him we hadn't realised just how low the speed limit was and he let us off. We pulled in at some shops to ask where Al and Fran lived, and they told us to turn left out of the car park and take the first left 100 yards along. The roads were quite and what did we do? Yes, we turned left onto the left-hand side of the road. We should have got away with it as it was a quiet Sunday morning, but we had no sooner turned than two pickup trucks came over the brow of the hill, side by side racing each other. I put my hands over my head and ducked. John said they passed one on each side of us. It was a good job there were wide grassy sides for them to do this or it could have been nasty. We had a lovely lunch with Al and Fran and they took us to see their small pier were, if they wanted, they could launch a boat onto a man-made lake which had been built for water storage for Shreveport which is on the Texas, Louisiana border. We haven't been back to the states since. We kept in touch with the family although Al died within a year of our visit and Fran died two years later. Al had stated in his will that he wanted his body donated for science but they didn't want it and poor Fran had to deal with finding another home for it. When we visited

Fran gave me a cow-shaped milk jug as a gift which I still have. It was made in China and the poor cow only has three teats but I always think of Al and Fran when I dust it.

A young American girl booked in with us for two nights and told us she was travelling round Europe before settling down to find a job. She had breakfast on the first morning and said she was walking down to visit St. Winfried's Holy Well. She didn't return that evening and was still not back after breakfast the next morning. As a mother myself I worried as to what had happened to her travelling on her own. I checked her room and, in the end, later in the morning, I rang the police as I felt that if something had happened to her and I had done nothing they would want to know why I hadn't rung them. Two police officers came and looked through her room for clues at which point, now passed lunch time, she turned up. She couldn't believe that someone had cared enough to ring the police. She said that she went into Chester and met some 'people' and crashed in their house for the night without telling anyone. I do hope she learnt a lesson there about keeping people informed.

CHAPTER 6
DIRECTIONS.

Directions to Greenhill were a bone of contention over the years. It didn't matter which way I wrote signs or explained directions it was always the wrong way and always my fault. Some people just can not follow directions. Some people don't even know what make of car they are driving. A party of Americans had booked in and when they got to Holywell that evening one of them rang me for directions, well after the third phone call my husband told them to stay where they were, and he would drive up to meet them. He asked what sort of car they were driving, and they told him it was a red Ford. When he got there it wasn't even a Ford it was a Volkswagen. We often had to ask people where they were and drive up to find them and get them to follow us back to the farm.
At St. Winifred's Holy Well our sign read; 'Drive 200 yards and then turn left opposite the Royal Oak pub. Many a guest would turn left up the lane opposite the Well and up to our neighbour's farm to be greeted by a large number of barking dogs as the owners were dog breeders. It was also a difficult place to turn around if you didn't want to face the dogs and open the gate it meant a long

reverse downhill. Often our Bed and Breakfast visitors would stop and ask local people where Greenhill Farm was but that didn't always help as the locals would just send them to the farm they knew, it could be any of a dozen local farms in the area.

Our lane was single track and a gentleman from London asked what we did if we met a car on the road as he couldn't reverse. He told us that he drove out of his road in a morning to travel over London Bridge to work and he drove in the other end of the road at night to park up outside his house. He took a route which meant he didn't have to reverse.

Other guests would drive up the lane and swing left to follow the tarmac as the last piece of road was just stone and not made up with tarmac. It's amazing how many people can't reverse, when you have done a milk round you quickly learn how to drive through small spaces both backwards and forwards as when you are out first thing in the morning there are cars parked everywhere in housing estates, some very close together. If you met the postman, another delivery driver or early riser you often had to reverse for considerable distances. On the milk round one morning I had parked to deliver some milk when another car came up the road and the drive shouted to me to move as he couldn't get his car through the gap. There was plenty of room and I wasn't in the mood to be polite. I told him he could get his car through the gap but he said he couldn't, so I told him to get out and I'd drive his car through the gap. The upshot was that he drove his car through without me having to move the pickup.

A London couple wrote to book a week stay, the envelope was addressed to Greenhill Farm, Bryn Celyn, Holywell, Clwyd. I replied addressing the letter from Greenhill Farm, Bryn Celyn, Holywell, Clwyd and enclosed a copy of my brochure which included my street map of the area. At about 5pm I got a phone call from the couple asking me for directions. I asked were they where and they gave me the name of a pub I had never heard of which confused me. The couple then asked some people in the pub and I could clearly hear laughing in the background. They had actually driven to Holywell in Cornwall. I didn't wait up for them, they took it all in good spirit, I never found out if they found somewhere to stay but I lost a booking. People don't realise that if they don't turn up I have lost my income. Often it is too late to relet the room.

This happened again when a family of four booked in by telephone and later rang for directions. They had also driven to Holywell in Cornwall. This time the wife was none too pleased, her response was, 'What am I going to tell my husband' 'what are we going to do now' and 'where are we going to sleep tonight'. I couldn't really answer any of these questions and again I didn't wait up for them. It was a relief when our address reverted back to being Flintshire. There are apparently four or five Holywell's in the UK.

As the lane to the farm was so narrow people often would ring from the phone box at the end of the road to check where we where. One evening a guest rang me and I asked her where she was, it's no good giving directions if you don't know where you are directing from. She looked across from the phone box at the lane running up hill in front of her and promptly said: 'It can't be up there all farms are on the level'. Well that was the first I knew about that especially living in Wales famous for its hills.

The people who were best at understanding directions were airline pilots, followed by members of the military; they must have been well trained at map reading. The average person couldn't even read a map, and this was well before the advent of satellite navigation systems. But even that wasn't much help. Guests would either drive up and down the Greenfield road or, if they managed to turn up our lane half way up they would swing left because that was where there was tarmac, our stretch was not tarmaced, when they turned left it lead to a terraced row of eighteen houses and was only a single track road, the only way out was to reverse all the way. The post code covered all the houses in Bryn Celyn which was over forty homes. One night John had to go and reverse a lady's car for her because she couldn't reverse out of the side lane. When in 2008 we finally got our 'new' road into a local housing estate we had to change the direction on the web site and, although our address had one post code we clearly stated that guests must use the other post code belonging to the house by the new entrance, to find us. This totally confused people. They couldn't believe you got to a farm through a housing estate.

My experiences with guests lead me to always have a pen and paper in our car so that if I needed directions I could write them down. John has a Westfield kit car and, when we are out with the club we always carry a map in the car. Most of the members don't, relying on their mobile phones but this doesn't always work when out in the countryside on back lanes. On one occasion I was left to look after a broken-down kit car parked in a lay by. The other car had to take the driver back down the mountain to get mobile reception to ring a recovery company after consulting our map to be able to tell the company exactly where he was.

Our Direction problems were increased in June 2003 when the road leading up to the farm collapsed. We had been away for the weekend and came home to find that a builder down the road had dug out his site to make it bigger. The site was below the road and he had left the road exposed to the elements. There had been a thunder storm and heavy rain while we were away and the soil under the road had been washed away. At that time the bulk tank lorry which collected the milk came in every other day and so we had forty-eight hours to sort out another route. The powers that be told us that we crossed the road at our own risk. At first, they were not very helpful but when they found over thirty houses trapped they were forced to act. The law says that access must be found for ambulances and fire engines if more than twenty-five houses are trapped. We owned the strip of land between the farm and the housing estate which had been built in the late nineteen eighties, known as Tan-y-Felin. Firstly, we needed access for our milk lorry and secondly, we knew and were friends with all our neighbours who were trapped and so we gave permission to the Highways Department of Flintshire County Council to make a road across our strip of land and along a public footpath to join up with the original road. We and our neighbours all thought that the council would come in and re build the road but no this wasn't to be. The law says that if a road collapse is above the road the council has to repair the problem but if a collapse is below the road it is the land owner's problem to make the road safe. This led to discussions with the land owner to which none of the locals were invited or informed about. The land owner had outlying planning permission to build a house on the plot but not detailed permission. Apparently, a deal was done in which he had permission to build his house with a retaining wall attached to it to hold the road up. In the mean time our milk lorry and cattle feed delivery lorries had to reverse up the newly made road so that they could then drive forwards up our road to the farm. This was viable for a few days but not long term. We needed a road across our field to join into the new estate as we were told that the house build was not going to be finished for some time. The Highways department were so good with us; they came in and built a road across the field. They first had to send an environmental inspector out who wasn't happy that we had to take out a gate width of hawthorn hedge but the lovely man from the Highways department had 'words' with him and all was sorted amicably. They also had to put new sign's up at the end of the Tan-y-Felin road and diversion signs everywhere to help people to find us all. This did cause some fun and games one day when there was a fire on the Flint to Prestatyn coast road which the police had to close and direct people up the Well Hill past our diversion signs. The problem was that people kept following all the diversion signs and ended up in our yard! Eventually the builder built his house and the old road was reopened. At this point the Planning Department informed us that they wanted the road across the field removed and so, because it had proved so much safer than the original road we applied for planning permission for the road. The residents of the cul-d-sac through which the road passed objected vigorously along with the local councillor and our first application was refused but it took nine months for the council to come to a decision. As the planning application our advisor had put in was a simple one because we hadn't foreseen any problems our next application had to be up to the standard needed to take to appeal in the Welsh Office if we were refused again. Sure enough five months later our second application was refused. Not only that but the council threatened to take us to court to make us remove the road that they had built at their expense with their permission. Who are these people? We always did have the backing of the Highways department but, apparently the Highways Department and the Planning Department didn't see eye to eye. We then applied under the appeal system to the Welsh Office and eventually in May 2007 they passed our appeal but we had to wait to use the road as the locals continued to block it with their cars until we had paid Flintshire County Council to drop the kerb. And so in August 2007, four years after the saga began, we officially had our new road and could plan properly to advertise it. The old road was still open because the Welsh Office said we could keep it open, we had always offered to close it and only use one entrance so in the end we were better off that when the saga started because one greedy man wanted to make his building plot bigger. We are not sure if the retaining wall, attached to the house, is built up to standard but we now have another entrance if anything happens in the future. Having two entrances didn't always help us, the new road was safer and easier to use but this meant that on the web site we had two Post Codes. Our house post code, on our address page and the Post Code for the house neared the new entrance which was on the Directions page of the web site. People still got confused or didn't read the directions page or not even copy it to take with them on their journeys.

During this time we had a guest staying who had also had a planning problem which had dragged on and on in England. He told us that he was building an industrial unit and the planners had put one obstacle after another in front of him. They made him build a bank between the industrial unit and the road to hide it and to top it all off they asked him for a list of the plants he was going to plant on the bank. This was the final straw and so he made up a list of plants using their Latin names which the council passed. The Latin names translated as dandelions, nettles, buttercups etc. We congratulated him on his imagination and on winning his case. Anyone who had tried to get planning permission will know how difficult it is.

CHAPTER 7
ADVERTISING.

Our very first 'adverts' were signs, near St. Winifred's Holy Well and at the end of the road, near the Royal Oak pub. One morning, when John was out delivering milk, he found that someone had shinned up the pole we had put our sign on and spray painted it over in black. Why would anyone really have a need to do that, I'll never know. Poor John had to paint a new sign. To avoid the same thing happening again, first he erected the new sign and then he covered the pole with thick globby tractor grease. Can you believe it, someone tried to climb the pole again using pieces of newspaper on the grease but John had done too good a job for them and the pieces of newspaper remained until the weather finally did for them. The sign wasn't vandalised again, we never found out who really did not want us to have our advert there. It seemed rather petty as it didn't do anyone any harm. Local signposting became a problem in later years as the local authority would make us take them down if we didn't have planning permission, but permission was almost impossible to get. It was so bad that eventually the Flintshire Tourism

Association, of whom I was one of the founder members, organised a meeting between us, the Planning Department and the Highways Department as they both had different rules. If you asked planning what the requirements where and put in an application, you would have it refused because it didn't comply with highways and vice versa. We did our homework and eventually got them to make a joint list of requirements to make it easier for people to apply. I did once, in frustration ring the councils Trading Standards Department and tell them I was having trouble with an organisation who wanted money up front with no guarantee I would get what I wanted. They got very excited, yes they were the people who could help me, until I told them it was their Planning Department, they soon backed off. Its fine for Councils to take your money and not deliver the goods but it's not fine for businesses.

One of the important parts of advertising is the quality of the pictures in the adverts. Although I have taken many of my own pictures I also used a local lady called Miss Beech who, with her brother, ran a toy shop and photography business in Holywell. They had a wonderful toy shop, stacked to the rafters of every toy you could ever want. For passport photos you had to squeeze up the stairs between the boxes to a small corner in a box filled room were the pictures would be taken. She took the pictures for Jennifer's wedding and, somehow, don't ask me how, her brother managed to be in most of the pictures taken outside Holywell's St. James's Church. I often had her take pictures of both inside and outside of the house as she had a much better camera and was better at the job than I would ever be.

Over the years I have used a number of advertising companies. Early on in my career, in an age before computers, after first using the 'Stay on a Farm' book, we would often go to book shops, trawl the shelves for B&B books and ask the staff which books sold the best, this lead to us joining the Welsh Tourist Board. They would send us the required literature with the grading structure for inspection and membership. Originally someone would ring and make an appointment before inspecting us but this altered over the years, first there would be a spot check and then an overnight stay. All of which we paid for in our membership fee. As well as the membership fee we had to pay a ten percent fee on every booking that a tourist information office sent us. Every year the 'to do' list would alter, in my opinion, to justify their jobs. I did the job for so many years I could often work out if a booking was being made by an inspector; I got to know their voices. Some were better than others, if I wasn't happy with an inspection I would complain. On one particular occasion I was in the office talking to an inspector when a guest knocked on the office door to ask if they could have an evening meal that evening. I apologised and said that it was too late to book dinner that night but, if they wanted one, I could make dinner the following night for them. The inspector put in his report that I didn't provide evening meals! He couldn't have been deaf as he'd heard the first part of the conversation but ignored the second part. About 5 years later he arrived again and had the cheek to ask if I remembered him as he was the inspector I'd complained about, he certainly hadn't forgotten.

One of the early inspections took place when an inspector would ring first to make an appointment. One year the inspector rang up and I apologised an explained that we were going away on holiday that week and could he please give me another date. He said he would ring again when he was back in the area. When we went away on this occasion a girl called Alex was milking for us and so it was arranged for her to stay in the house and to look after the dogs. One morning there was a knock on the front door and who should be there but the Tourist Board Inspector. Alex, very sensibly explained that we were away and that, as she was only the milk maid, she didn't feel as though she should show him around and could he please call again when we returned. This was another occasion when I complained about an inspector, I felt that he was virtually accusing me of lying to him on the phone. That I'd used 'going away' as an excuse not to have him come; this I felt was wrong on his part and told the Tourist Board in no uncertain terms.

As part of our Tourist Board membership we not only had an advert in the Tourist Board literature we had the use of the Tourist Information Offices. I got to know many of their local staff well and even those from further afield, especially when Holyhead Information office had been given good report of my accommodation and rang me up with customers regularly. I was only about an hours drive from the ferry port. Our nearest TIC was based in a caravan at Halkyn, by the Little Chef on the A55 but this eventually closed in 1988 and moved into Mold where it continued in the Library until the year after we retired. There is now no TIC in Flintshire to my knowledge although a number of local attractions and local libraries have deliveries of brochures for the North Wales area from a company called North Wales Tourism.

We also joined the AA to enable us to go into their B&B book; it was a very successful arrangement for many many years. They had some really lovely inspectors. I did have an embarrassing moment with an inspector when I was having my mid-life crisis. I was in the middle of the menopause which caused me to flush for no apparent reason. This happened one day while I was talking to an AA inspector. I apologised and explained why I was blushing so and he replied. 'And I thought you liked me'. How embarrassing, I think he was also embarrassed and thought that was the best thing to say.

One particular fetish for all Inspectors was coat hangers. There had to be a minimum of four hangers per person per room, some of which had to be suitable to hang trousers on and they all had to match. The metal coat hangers that you get from the dry cleaners where a no no, never must they be seen in a guest house wardrobe. I had a varied selection, wooden in the best rooms and strong plastic in other rooms, some black, some grey or white. Well coat hangers had a perchance for walking. Don't ask me how but the colours never matched up in the rooms. I spent a great deal of time moving coat hangers around rooms. When people arrived with their own hangers I think they would get mixed up and go home with mine leaving their own, and when a couple had children in another room I think they moved by accident, but it never really explained how all the coat hangers moved so regularly. I ended up convinced that, during the night, they would squeeze through key holes and dance around the landing and in their rush to get back to a wardrobe when they heard a noise, they would go through the wrong key hole back to the wrong room.

Two years after we retired we stayed in a hotel near Southampton as it was convenient to visit friends. When we booked the room we were told that they only had Superior rooms left but the location suited us and so we booked the more expensive Superior room. Yes it was beautiful and expensive but not only didn't it have a suitcase stand, another 'must have', it only had 2 coat hangers. It was one of the rare occasions when I did complain, mainly I don't as we can all make minor mistakes but if everything else is fine you can forgive. I complained because when we asked for a suit case holder as we didn't have one the hotel manager didn't believe us and insisted on inspecting the room himself and making a fuss as to what a beautiful room it was and how an overseas princess had stayed and loved the room. I'm afraid he put my back up I made out a list of problems that I found with the room including extremely bad lighting in the bathroom, so bad that they had put in a 50x magnified mirror. When you get to a certain age you really don't want to scc yoursclf in a 50x magnified mirror, it does nothing for you confidence. Also the bedroom mirror was set too high for me to see into when I sat at the dressing table, I can't be the only 5foot 2 ½ inch tall customer they had ever had.

Another thing the inspectors insisted on was cups and saucers and a teapot in the bedrooms. In one room I had mugs as decorations, on top of the pelmets over the curtains. Often guests would take these down to use as they where not used to cups and saucers at home. Most people these days use mugs. I told the inspectors that the time would come when only mugs where used both at the table and in the rooms and, sure enough, in 2009 Hilton Hotels used mugs on their breakfast tables. In later years I would often have young workmen who didn't put cups back on saucers although the French often didn't either. Eventually I put mugs into all the bedroom as my customers much preferred to use mugs.

In the early years voucher schemes where fashionable, they were used by the AA, the Tourist Board, a company called Pilgrims Progress along with Wayfares and Country Rovers. All these schemes where very successful at bringing in customers for a period of time in the 1980's. The idea was that the customer, booked accommodation from lists the package included a hire car; a sort of package holiday with the freedom to stay where you wanted. This was especially liked by overseas customers who could plan their journeys in advance. They paid the voucher company up front and the company paid us after the visit. Customers would often fly into Heathrow airport and pick up a hire car. They would then travel around the UK and often stay with me the night before they travelled over to Ireland on the Holyhead ferry. The thing that really worried them was that, when they left their hire car in the car park in Holyhead the hire company told them just to lock up the car and put the keys in the exhaust pipe. I don't know how well this worked for the hire company, but it did seem a bit dangerous, I often wondered if they ever had a car stolen.

We did have a family to stay who tried to get their money back off the voucher company when they went home early. It was a German family who arrived in the early afternoon. In those days you greeted them with a cup of tea and cakes which I duly did. I could tell that they were unhappy about something; but often customers could be tired after travelling all day but would be much happier the next morning. They sat on the edge of their chairs and their whole body language read, 'not happy'. I showed them their room and all was well as far as I was concerned. The next morning they didn't come down for breakfast. When I checked their room they had left in the night. I rang the company and explained what had happened and told them that the family had not been very chatty the night before. They told me not to worry and that they would pay me as they had already been paid and the guests had used the beds. Two months later the guests wrote to the company and complained about my accommodation saying they had to leave as it was so bad. The company rang me up to arrange a visit. They came and inspected me and where quite happy with everything. I had done a lot of business with them and this was the only complaint they had had about my accommodation. They told me that someone must have put it into the guest's heads that, if they complained, they might get their money back for the stay as they had gone home early. I know this is done but it isn't very nice for the accommodation providers who are doing their best.

That was the first of only three complaints in thirty-five years in the job. The second was a couple who had booked in to go to a wedding. Their son fetched them up to the farm and they were not happy chatty people. They told me that someone was going to collect them to take them to the wedding. I was gardening near the front door when they came out ready to be collected. I tried very hard to make polite conversation with little success. When their lift arrived, it turned out to be the father of a friend of our daughters who was happy to pass the time of day. The next morning when they came down for breakfast they came to speak to me. They said that the wardrobe in their bedroom had fallen on them and that the husband had been injured. I apologised and said I couldn't understand how it happened. After breakfast they said they would be going for a walk as their son was not to pick them up for an hour. They went out and walked for at least three quarters of an hour. He really couldn't have been that badly injured. I went up to the bedroom and found that the wedge under the wardrobe had been removed. You have to remember that this is a very old house, none of the floors are level and wedges where used under beds to level them and, in this case, under one side of the front leg of the wardrobe. I tried to pull the wardrobe over with no wedge and found that it only swayed slightly if you pulled it when the door was open. When the door was shut the wardrobe was stable. It was very difficult to actually pull the wardrobe over, the wedges where just a precaution. Within two days I received a solicitor's letter threatening me. I handed it over to our insurance company with all the details. The trouble is that people get away with these complaints because it is cheaper and easier for the insurance company to pay out than it is to fight the case when it's obvious to me that they were just trying it on. It wouldn't surprise me, given their unwillingness to communicate with me from the word go, if they hadn't decided to try it on before they arrived to defray the costs of going to a wedding. People who do this don't realise how upsetting it is for a small business to be accused of something when they are doing their very best to provide good service and make their customers happy.

The third complaint was rather silly really, but the guests tried to blow it up into something serious. Two ladies had asked Llangollen Tourist Information Centre to book them into the nearest accommodation to St. Winifred's Holy Well. That was my guest house and so they arrived on a warm, dry autumn day after my husband had been spreading slurry. You have to remember that the main point of their visit was to go to the Well, not to visit a farm. The first lady stepped out of the car and smelt the slurry. It showed on her face, she was not impressed. Once someone isn't happy they will find everything they can to complain about. I showed them up to my best room in the oldest part of the house. It has oak beams throughout and its own bathroom with a shower over the bath. In-between the black oak beams the walls it was painted with Magnolia emulsion paint. To set off the black and white the bed throws and curtains were in matching red. The bathroom has a front view over the river and beyond and the bedroom itself overlooks my beautiful garden, awash with colourful plants with my vegetable garden next to the shed and then over the town of Holywell with the Holy Well in the for ground. They rang the bell a number of times. Firstly, they had had showers and wanted to dry their towels but the radiators where cold, it was a warm day, do you really want the radiators blasting out heat? I explained that there was a dryer available in the utility room for the use of guests or that I would give them clean towels if they would prefer it. The next morning they said that they had to move on although they were booked in for two nights. My first thoughts where, 'thank God for that' but I smiled sweetly and took their money. As I said, this was in the September. In late January I received a letter from the Welsh Tourist Board informing me that I'd had a complaint made against me and my accommodation. They sent me a copy of the letter which was very long. They mentioned the turned off radiators and the fact that it was so hot they had to leave the bedroom windows open even with the smell of sheep in the sheds. They said that the carpet was thread bare; it was a 3 year old Wilton carpet with no wear on it at all. They mentioned that under the mattress there were wooden planks holding the bed up, this is nothing unusual on some modern beds. This was an antique oak bed which had originally had big springs under it. Our girls had had hours of fun bouncing on it but the downside was that it squeaked. This is not ideal for guests; no one wants to listen to a squeaky bed though the wall when they want to sleep and its embarrassing for the inmates of the bed. I won't elaborate on that. The list went on and on, they even complained that I didn't give a genuine smile when they told me they where only staying one instead of two nights. Well I say 'they' it was mainly the ring leader of the two ladies, the other lady just seemed to tag along.

When a complaint is made to the Tourist Board their procedure is to send a copy to the accommodation provider, wait for their reply and forward this on to the complainant. Generally no further action is taken and I expect that this is what happened to my reply in which I commented on each point individually. I did explain that we only spread slurry after we had finished harvesting our grass to make silage and that the smell was a short-term problem which came with farming. I also explained that our literature fully states we are a dairy farm and have no sheep at all. Every comment was answered and I did apologise for not looking genuinely happy when I was smiling through gritted teeth. I thought that would be the end of the matter. A couple more months went by; it must have been in about March. I was happily doing a pile of ironing and listening to the radio. I'm one of those strange people who love ironing, with a cup of coffee by my side and the radio to listen to I find it really relaxing. The 'phone in' that day was for funny experiences guests had had in guest houses and bed and breakfasts. Well I just had to listen to that didn't I? One couple had stayed in a guest house in Scotland where the land lady told them that if they wanted a bath they must ask her for the key to unlock the bath taps. They duly asked for a bath and she went up to their room, ran the bath for them and locked the taps before leaving. Another couple had had the misfortune of the fire alarms going off in the middle of the night only to find that their room had the fire escape in it and as they sat up in bed other guests dashed through the room to escape. There were some really amusing stories but when the announcer introduced the last story I recognised the voice straight away; yes it was the lady who didn't like the smell of slurry. She proceeded to tell the presenter how disgusting it was to have to stay somewhere with the smell of slurry and that I shouldn't be allowed to be in business. Before she could continue the presenter butted in. He must have been a country lover as he calmly told her that if she stayed in the countryside she should expect to accept the country ways and promptly cut her off. I felt vindicated.

I did have a guest who spent her whole weekend complaining to me. She didn't go on to complain to anyone else but gave us a very busy weekend. Complaint number one was lack of blankets on the bed; she hadn't even looked in the wardrobe where we kept an extra blanket for guests who needed them. Some of the Americans from the Deep South would feel the cold in the UK and so I kept an extra blanket in every bedroom. Next complaint was that the front room was cold and so we just lit the fire for her but she certainly kept us running round. Keeping the house at the right temperature to please everyone was a problem which was exasperated when the oil prices went through the roof. It would have cost me over a hundred pounds a week to keep the temperature of the house up all the time. This wasn't viable if we only had one or two guests staying. We farmers are a hardy breed and well used to adding an extra cardigan but most people now live in small modern houses were they can afford to keep the temperatures high. At breakfast the next morning her mushrooms weren't cooked enough. How can you under cook a mushroom when it can be eaten raw. This complaint really upset Susan who was waiting on table; she'd never had anyone complain to her before. I politely cooked some more and sent them through on a plate and she was happy. We just carried on and smiled through the complaints, but she certainly made heavy weather of her weekend away. I don't think she had wanted to go away in the first place.

Part of advertising is to keep a good reputation, half of my customers where repeat customers. Mr and Mrs Laverick from Northallerton in Yorkshire stayed with us on and off for 25 years. They were dairy farmers and their youngest son was a musician. At first they stayed when holidaying in North Wales and then as they were passing through to see their youngest son at University in Cardiff where he trained to be a music teacher. Our middle daughter, Jennifer played the cornet for a while and our youngest daughter, Clare played both the saxophone and the tenor horn, she went on to teach me music and I've been playing in bands for a number of years on a tenor horn, cornet and lately, a trumpet. One July evening they arrived up unexpectedly when we were going out for dinner as we had no other guests in at the time, so they joined us at the Brookhouse Mill near Denbigh. This is, as the name suggests, a converted mill which has served as a pub for too many years to remember. It is owned and run by someone who was born and brought up local to us in Holywell and has always had a good reputation. The Brookhouse were doing a special offer which none of us could resist, it was for a steak dinner followed by strawberries and cream. We all ordered this and it was delicious, made even more so when the waitress got herself all confused because we were arguing over who was paying and she only charged us for two meals in stead of four. We all had a lovely evening, another satisfied customer. We also visited the Laverick's on their dairy farm when we were in Yorkshire.

Another part of advertising is improving the quality of the accommodation by doing courses. I have done various courses which usually end up with another certificate for the wall. In 1993 the Tourism Association subsidised members to complete the Welcome Host course which I renewed in 2000 and received a Gold Standard. In 2003 I had a certificate for taking part in 'Hospitable Climates' working to reduce energy in the hospitality industry. Also in 2003 I completed a Presentation and

Speaking Skills Workshop which gave me yet another certificate. In 2004 I had a certificate for Wales Environment Awards, encouraging businesses not to waste energy etc. We also entered a HSBC North Wales tourism competition and came runner up which led to a big write up in the local paper. In 2009 I joined the committee of Holywell's 'Walkers are Welcome' town which led to more pictures in the local paper.

We always took a magazine called Moneywise in which they do money makeovers for people and we were featured in the August 1993 edition. They sent a financial advisor to work with us and a photographer came to picture us on the farm. John and I were pictured in the magazine with the advisor and with our pedigree bull. Clare was about 6 years old and she had her picture taken by our house sign holding a huge cooked breakfast. The upshot from this was that the photographer contacted us to see if he could use Clare's picture for a centre spread in the Observer newspaper when they where doing an accommodation article. Of course I said yes hoping to get some business from the article. I only had one enquiry and I was full on the dates they wanted. It just goes to show that advertising is an odd thing; you just never know what works and what doesn't work so you just try everything. I always had an advertising budget which seemed to rise every year but was a necessity for us as we were not on the roadside were everyone could see a sign.

As I advertised in the Chester Visitors Guide I was invited to a talk by Chester Tourism in the grounds of Chester Zoo. In Flintshire we work off the back of Chester for a lot of our tourism business. When we got to the 'any questions' part of the day I did ask why they hadn't mentioned Flintshire as the county border comes within a mile of the city walls. Apparently there is still a law which says that if any Welsh person is seen from the city walls after dust they could be killed. Since we voted for a devolved government in Wales it's been as if a huge brick wall has materialised between us and England. It became even worse a few years later when the UK government reorganised the North of England boundaries and gave Warrington control of tourism in the North West. Up to that point we had had a very constructive relationship between Chester and Flintshire Tourism Departments. I had my polite reply and after the meeting a gentleman approached me and told me he was from the local radio station, Dee 106. He gave me the opportunity to put together a few words advertising Flintshire. I went home and, with trepidation, put pen to paper. On the allotted day I turned up at the radio station and recorded my piece to be broadcast across the Chester area. I think it took me about three attempts to get it right but they were all very patient with me. It was my only time in a radio station and one to add to my experiences.

From the late 1980's onwards there where a number of Agricultural grants to encourage farmers to modernise and to use computers and so in the autumn of 1992 I joined a computer course along with a number of local farmer's wives. I was already a touch typist which made it easier for me to follow a computer screen as I didn't have to keep looking down at the key board. This course meant a one evening a week drive up to Denbigh where the course was held during the winter months. I had the furthest to travel to Denbigh, it took me about thirty minutes on a good run, but I knew the course would benefit me greatly. I didn't have a computer myself and had to go and visit a friend in the local housing estate to do my 'homework' for the course which led to a Royal Society of Arts (RSA) qualification if I passed. My friend Wendy was good enough to let me use her husband's computer when he was at work. Half way through the course the teacher 'did a runner'. Apparently she'd had boyfriend problems which had blown up into a big deal and she'd just 'done a runner' and disappeared with the computers. The organisers where obliged to find a replacement course which they managed to do just down the road from the farm in Greenhill, so very convenient for me. I signed up straight away but none of the other farmers wives bothered so I carried on quietly on my own until I passed my RSA and was awarded a certificate in 1994 at a presentation evening hosted by our local council. It was a memorable afternoon, the certificates were first handed out and then we had speeches by the staff and a local councillor followed by a buffet for the certificate recipients and their families. This was great not only because of the experience but because the new teachers taught all sorts of courses and where able to give me some good advice about local grants. From this I applied for a small business grant which paid fifty percent for computers, office equipment and other goods which could improve my business. Included in the computer grant were a number of hours with a business and computer adviser called Susan. I invested in a computer and some office furniture which I'm still using to this day. We also had some garden chairs and a big children's swing to replace the swing on a Black Poplar tree in the orchard/children's play area as it had fallen down.

We tried to encourage people to take an interest in the animals by providing safe standing room in the milking parlour as a viewing gallery but not all the children were prepared to stand still and watch. Parents would stand and ask all sorts of questions which John would patiently answer, but some children would loss interest quickly and try to get up to mischief and try and get onto tractors and machinery. We didn't want to be cross with guests and so we fenced off a corner of the field next to the house and made an orchard come play area where we put the swings and seating. It was a lovely spot overlooking the river and we planted a hawthorn hedge around it with apple, damsons and cherry trees. Into this area we also planted a hundred weight of daffodil bulbs which were beautiful in the spring. We also planted daffodil bulbs up each side of the road leading up to the farm.

The best part of this grant was Susan, who showed me how to use the internet to advertise. She showed me how to search under different criteria for accommodation in our area and then I could see which 'advert' where coming up on the first two pages of Google and then join those advertisers. At first you could scroll to the bottom of a page and find out how to contact the company and, more often than not, get a free listing as they wanted your trade as much as you wanted theirs. This way of advertising gave us smaller accommodation providers a much better chance of reaching the wider population and it did wonders for the business, increasing trade considerably. She taught me all about security on the net and told me I needed a website of my own. I used a company which employed one of my guests and they sold me a domain name and built me a website with a notice board as one of the pages on it were I could add my own stories, pictures and vacancy date. The first page of my web site was all about our accommodation, the farm, the views and the local attractions. I could update the Notice Board myself to put on any relevant information such as if we were full, what was on in the area, pictures of the animals, especially any new baby calves, or puppy dogs and of the garden. Later on, when John bought his Westfield Kit Car, we looked into hiring it out to guests but this was going to be a problem with insurance so we put some information on the Notice Board page saying that, if they paid for the fuel, John would give them an hour's drive in the car. It gave him a chance to wind down after work, for free. This proved very popular with both sexes. One girl asked me if I screamed when he went fast, I said no, he needed to concentrate on his driving. He is a good driver having done some midnight car rallying before we met but he did manage to spin the car one day – not with a guest but with me as passenger, he hit the inside bank of a corner trying to keep up with one of the club's wilder drivers and when we stopped spinning I was only a couple of feet away from a 30 foot drop and I didn't scream once! We did tell the children that when life was no longer fun we would drive over a cliff in the car, there reply was: 'What a waste of a good car, get out and jump'. John took one man out who was a ukelele player. After the ride he made us take his picture sat on the back of the car with his instrument he was so pleased. I am one of the few wives to go out in the kit car regularly although I don't drive it; I have no problem with the speed. In fact one day we had been out the night before and I wouldn't let John drive until after 12pm as he'd had a couple of drinks. We were in the BMW Z4 that day as the Westfield was in for a service and one of the younger drivers commented that I might drive too slow as we were leading that day. Drive too slow, I managed to loose them all, the road we were on was one I drove regularly to the Cash and Carry, I knew where every gear change was. They don't complain any more in fact they now call me 'Scary Mary'.

We also had to have an Access page on the website which explained what facilities, if any, we had for various disabilities. I had to say how many steps there where into the house etc. As our house was so old we couldn't take anyone in a wheelchair. My own mother was in a wheel chair for the last few years of her life and she couldn't visit us very often. Firstly the space between the stairs and a wall was so narrow a chair wouldn't go through from the guest's front room to any other rooms in the house. The stairs were a later addition to the house when an upstairs floor was put in. Secondly, because of the layout of the house and as part of the house was below ground level, we couldn't install a downstairs toilet.

On the website I had a 'booking' page which people making enquires could fill in and email to me. I could then forward them either by email or brochure, further information as per their needs. Just occasionally someone with nothing else to do would fill the page with rubbish in all sorts of languages. On one occasion someone made an enquiry just for something to do and led me a merry dance with emails back and too until I realised and told him to politely ‘go away’. He threatened to have me blacklisted with all his friends. I thought that what a good idea of his to discourage his friends, I didn’t want his sort staying if they were just staying to cause trouble. At about this time one of my ‘regular’ customers and I became big friends. She was contracted to a local company for ten days a month. The company were willing to pay for her to stay in hotels but she wanted to stay in a B&B were it would be more homely and she wouldn’t have to sit on her own in a big dinning room every evening, and so she ended up with me. She was a web designer and programmer and so she wrote me a B&B accounts programme which linked pages together. When I filled in details on my ‘Money In’ page this would update other pages and so I could see which adverts brought in the most money and which were not working at all. This was a great help as advertising is an expensive job and you need to pick the right place. I was an early member of the Flintshire Tourism Association which had a big membership of all sorts of tourism operators. If I was full I would recommend someone else in the area and vice a versa. This worked very well as we all didn't use the same books or web pages to put adverts on. It meant we could cover a big area with our numbers. We kept business in Flintshire and guests were happy that we could recommend someone local to them.

During the late 1980's the business changed considerably. More people were going abroad for their holidays in the sun and more companies were using contract workers who needed accommodation for four nights a week while they where working away from home. Also new homes were smaller and if people had family to visit they didn't always have room to put them up and so needed local accommodation. At one point I did a local company and houses, leaflet drop. This was 1/3 A4 glossy paper with all my details on the front along with my AA and Wales Tourist Board ratings. On the back I did something a bit different, I got poetical. My effort read:

Here's somewhere to stay that's not far away.
For business or pleasure or on holiday.

Rooms with TV's and baths, in which to relax.
With prices we know will not overtax.
Where the pace of life is ever so calm.
To book a room just pick up the phone.
Whether you're with a friend or travelling alone.

I never found out if I got any customers from this leaflet but I hand delivered it door to door in the local housing estates and did have a lot of customers from the estates when family came to visit them.

One year a mystery advert for my accommodation appeared in the Lonely Planet Guide. Someone told me that I had an advert in this guide and so off I went to newsagents to look at the book and, low and behold, there I was in the North Wales section. I got in touch with the company to see how it had happened and, apparently their inspector just books in and stays for one or two nights and, if they like you you get put into the book. On my page it said that the proprietor had a good knowledge of the area and could tell you anything you needed to know. This was something that the Flintshire Tourism Association had discussed many years earlier and so the council organised for accommodation providers to have a local bus trip around the area telling us all the local history.

I had learnt a lot that day including the fact that Flint Castle has the tower with the thickest walls of any castle, twenty-three feet thick. When Henry Bolingbroke won the castle he had it partly demolished as it had been such a hard won battle he didn't want that problem again. A number of local houses are built in the stone taken from the castle.

Another interesting fact we learnt was that the bullet marks in Mold's old Town Hall were caused when the local Militia tried to quell a riot. The story goes like this: there were a number of mines in the Mold area and a new manager was brought in from Durham. He wasn't popular with the Welsh miners and this was exasperated when he tried to ban the use of the Welsh Language at work. This was followed up with an announcement that he was going to cut their wages. The miners held a meeting, after which they marched on the manager's home, beat him up, emptied his house and took the furniture to the railway station as encouragement for him to go back to Durham. Seven men were arrested and stood trial in Mold Magistrate court, held in the

Town Hall, were they were sentenced to a month in prison. A big crowd had gathered outside the court but the authorise had anticipated this and had a large contingent of police on hand as well as a detachment of soldiers from the fourth regiment of the King's Own from the barracks at Chester. Two of the miners were fetched out of the court to be taken to jail at Flint but the crowd of over a thousand miners and their families reacted by hurling stones and missiles at the guards. The soldiers retaliated without warning killing four people, two of whom were women, and injuring many more. The crowd quickly dispersed. An inquest into the deaths gave a verdict of 'Justifiable Homicide', as under the Riot Act not more than twelve people could congregate but this was questionable because the 'Riot Act' should have been read out before the shooting began and it wasn't.

As well as the adverts we also had small notices in every bedroom with the meal times, booking in and booking out times on it along with our facilities, where the bell to call us was etc. Later on we also had notices in the bathrooms asking guest to put used towels in the bath and listing our Environmental endeavours both inside and out on the farm. We had been short listed for an Environmental Award but didn't win it as all our efforts where quite small really. On the farm John used old newspapers put through a straw chopping machine for the cows to lie on, before that he collected the shavings left over from the workshop in Courtaulds factory (long since gone) down the road. We found that very few people actually read these notices and I would be answering the bell to guests when, if they had read the notices they wouldn't have needed to come down and ask me. In fact one guest I had was staying to visit a local company to advise them on any Environmental Savings the company could make. He did read the bathroom notice because he told me how impressed he was with it, BUT he didn't take any notice of it, he, on his own, managed to use every towel in the bathroom for each night of his stay leaving them on the floor and not in the bath as asked on the notice, he obviously didn't practise what he preached.

I did have a problem with someone else's advert in 2004. A lady had been bought a guest house in Chester by her father. She had put an advert in the Chester Visitors Guide, under the Guest House section the same section as I was in, in fact her advert was next to mine. She had failed to proof read the advert before it was put into the book. All the companies I worked with would let you see exactly what the advert consisted of before it was printed, and I learnt to read through them carefully. She hadn't done this and the mistake was that my telephone number was on my advert and on her advert. Her telephone number was missing. The first I found out about this was when someone rang up to book and asked if there was private parking. Parking can be a problem with town guest houses, some people really don't want to park on the street and who can blame them. It did lead to some strange conversations and to thc realisation that people really don't listen to what you are saying on the phone. The course I did in public speaking taught me that people hear a third, read a third and see a third of any information. That is why, if you go to a talk you will often hear it, see it on a screen and be given the facts on paper. One afternoon we were having problems with a really difficult calving and John told me to run and ring the vet, and to tell him it was an emergency and for the vet to come as quickly as he could. As I reached the back door I could hear the phone ringing so I dashed in and picked it up. Imagine the scene, I'm in wellingtons and overalls and up to my teeth in SH 1 T, calving is a messy job. The gentleman on the phone can hear me panting after my run and so I apologised and told him I was sorry that I was panting but I was in the middle of calving a cow. Remember that bit; I was in the middle of calving a cow. He asked for a double, ensuite room which I said I had, he asked the price and I took his details, name address phone number etc. Just as we were finishing the conversation he asked, by the way did I have private parking? Bells began to ring in my head; I'd heard this before so I asked him if he wanted Greenhill Farm or Grosvenor Guest House. Yes, you guessed, he wanted Grosvenor Guest House. How many cows do they calve in the middle of Chester you can ask, I really don't know. I eventually rang the vet who came and we had to give the cow a caesarean operation to bring out the calf alive. Mother and baby survived the experience. I got in touch with the lady who owned Grosvenor House and she was good enough to visit me with a bouquet of flowers for my trouble. This was when she admitted that she really didn't know what she was doing. The following year her advert wasn't in the book and I found out that she had gone out of business.

Over the years I saw a number of 'businesses' stop trading when they found out just how hard the job can be. At least two that I knew thought that guests would do things their way. No such luck, remember the rules:

Rule number one: The customer is always right.
Rule number two: When the customer is wrong remember rule number one.

Neither of these people lasted into their second years. I had spoken to both of them before they opened and it was obvious that in their eyes I knew nothing but it was them who knew nothing in the end. Others came and went over the years, one had a bad back and couldn't make the beds and one had her house compulsorily purchased by the Welsh Office to widen the A55. A scheme which hasn't as yet materialised. Some just found more lucrative or easier employment.

One thing that amused me over the year was people's attitude to prices. I always said that the Americans would knock at the door and say: 'Have you got a room?' The Europeans would knock at the door and ask 'Can I see the room?' and the British would knock at the door and say 'How much is the room?' There where always exceptions to this rule as I was reminded of one day when a German couple knocked on the door. I only had one double room left which I showed them. The bombastic husband then proceeded to stand on the landing and try and haggle down the price. He was rather brusk about it, it wasn't done in a nice way and it put my back up. I put my foot down with a firm hand and refused point blank to drop a penny and so they left. Later that day another couple came along and I let the room at my usual price. Staying at a Bed and Breakfast is the cheapest form of accommodation that you will find with everything included I thought it bad taste to try and knock the price down further. Only once did I not get paid, I learnt fast, what happened was the local post man who was also a friend had been asked by a couple if he knew were they could stay, without any more ado he loaded them up in his van and fetched them to me thinking he was doing me a good turn. These people had no money, I the end I let them stay the night and they left without paying me. I had a guest in sent by the company he was working for and they didn't pay me, I rang and rang but got no were so in the end I drove down to their factory and parked my car across they entrance and refused to move it until I was paid. They gave in and paid me out of the petty cash. A week or two later I got a letter from the receivers of the company which had gone into receivership and my name was on the creditors list. I was pleased I'd done what I did otherwise I might never had seen the money.

When we lived in Clwyd County Council our local council went under the name of Delyn Borough Council and this council formed a Tourism Association in the mid 1980's. I joined this association along with other local tourism businesses, hotels, caravan parks and attractions. We all worked together to promote the area and we recommended each other and so kept people in the area. If one of us was full and couldn't take a guest we would make sure we gave them the telephone number of one of our members, they were grateful and we kept business in Flintshire. When we went back to becoming Flintshire the Flintshire Tourism Association was formed working with the Tourism Officer for Flintshire County council. The officer, David Evans was glad of advice from the members and the members were glad to work with the council to promote the county. We had one of the few tourism associations in the country at that time. We put brochures together and, later on worked with Wrexham and Denbighshire to form the Borderlands area to produce even bigger better advertising. One year this brochure won an award for its creativity and good advertising. We would, through David, work with other departments in the council although we often found that planning permission especially for signs, was difficult so we arrange to meet with the Highways department and the Planning department to work out a list of requirements to help businesses to apply by giving them information before they started the process. All these things help to make life easier for all concerned. One of our members, Neil Evans, worked closely with David Evans to make a tourism route around the country show casing all the counties assets. It consisted of 84 miles of road and over 100 brown tourism signs. Highways insisted that the route turned left as much as possible as it would be safer and grant money was found to put all the signs up. One local gentleman I spoke to told me he was very worried when he saw sign number 60 going up outside his house, at first he thought it was a new speed sign! I sat on this committee for too many years to remember and was at various time both treasurer and chairperson.

During my time as Chair of the Association the talk in the country was for faster trains to London, especially the Virgin

Trains high speed Pendolino train. This train only came north up to Crewe and not along the line to Holyhead. This was of great concern to us in North Wales and so we contacted Virgin trains and they sent out a gentleman to talk to the association and to explain to us that the train couldn't stop at Flint because the station platform was too short for the number of carriages the train pulled. We also asked him about tourism adverts on the trains and I was especially interested in paper mats with local adverts on as I'd seen them all over Switzerland where a mats production and distribution system is run by their tourism departments. These mats can be seen on the tables of all eating establishments throughout the country. The gentleman told us that he'd been on a course about the mats put down for meals on the first-class carriages which had strawberries on them. When I asked why strawberries he said he didn't know because he'd fallen asleep during that part of the explanation! The upshot of the meeting was that he offered us free first-class ticket for the Virgin Pendolino trains; we just had to ring him and ask. A few months after this meeting a lady from the Mid Wales tourism association contacted us. Her friend was the local Liberal Member of Parliament and she'd been badgering him about the money spent in Wales on tourism which was as still is considerably less than that spent in England and Scotland. He'd agreed to have a meeting in Parliament for small Welsh businesses to go down and put their case to a range of parliamentary members from all parties. John and I agreed to go down to join her and so I rang up the nice man from Virgin and we where given 2 first class train tickets. Off we went to the meeting in Portcullis house, next door to the Houses of Parliament, with our official invitations. The whole day was a real eye opener. First class train travel was a first for us and then the plushness of Portcullis house and the buffet lunch served with bottles of 'House of Commons' wine. I did try and get an empty bottle to bring home as a souvenir but no such luck. The meeting itself was a bit of a disappointment. There were only about 3 liberal members their and no members from other parties. There was the chairman of the hotel tourism group who advise the government on UK tourism and then about ten or a dozen small business people from various tourism facilities throughout Wales. Lembit Opik chaired the meeting, and a good chairman he was to. He opened up the proceedings and when we asked questions he threw them at the hotel chairman who was total rubbish. He knew nothing about the tourism industry on the ground and we all had great fun shredding him to pieces. The meeting didn't produce anything of any substance for us but we did give the Liberal MPs a better understanding of what we needed as businesses. A few days later I rang the organiser and asked her about this hotel chairman, she told me she'd asked her MP and he said that they had heard from him previously and thought he was rubbish and so they just wanted to know how rubbish he was! This meeting just went to prove what I have always thought; you can actually be much more productive outside politics than inside. I have sat in various meeting with members of parliament down to local councillors and most of these organisations just seem to be talking shops.

Flintshire has a wealth of tourism potential but, because it isn't considered to be a poor county and has British Aerospace in its boundary tourism is only given lip service in my opinion. The local hospital, which had originally been a work house, then a hospital, now a listed building, was to be closed and our tourism association wrote to the Welsh Office suggesting that, as it was listed and must not be overly changed, it would make a good museum of nursing or the workhouse. We got a rather rude letter back to tell us that it was already sold for a fitness centre. That was over 10 years ago and the site is still not being used and deteriorating by the day.

CHAPTER 8
CORGI DOGS

Another website page we had was all about our corgi dogs.

John's family had always used corgis to round up the cattle. Corgis are Welsh Cow dogs, they run around the back of the cattle barking and nipping the ankles, when the cattle kick their feet they go over the dog's head. We had a number of Corgis over the years and we bred from them. Our first was Penny, registered name: Lady Penelope Jane which suited her well, her favourite game was to pick up and run off with the children's socks or toys, she would put them down and wait for you to reach for them before picking them up again and running off. This would continue for quite a while until she or we tired of the game. She gave us a number of puppy litters. We used our 'puppy money' to pay for our holidays. After Penny came Cindy who got to the mail before us one morning and chewed up a cheque for over a thousand pounds from the auctioneers after we sold some cattle, luckily there was enough left to see were it came from and I had to take it back and get another cheque. She was one of Penny's pups. This was followed by Candy who came along when Clare was about three years old, they were great friends. When Clare went to school Candy was lost and used to sit on the back-door step waiting for her to come home. Her favourite game was to push Clare off the bean bag when they shared it. She could wriggle and squirm across it until Clare rolled off it. When Clare was older she used to get so frustrated because Candy wouldn't obey her commands. As pack animals dogs have 'leaders' and pack members. John and I were 'leaders' but Clare was one of the pack. As Candy got older we decided we needed another puppy, we timed it so that we could breed in time for the Queens Silver Jubilee. Candy wasn't very well by now, she had had a number of cancerous growths removed and was very slow so we decided one pup may be too much for her as the pup would pester her and want to play with her, so we bought two, named by Clare to match Candy, we duly took ownership of Toffee and Fudge. They were not sisters, in fact they where like chalk and cheese. Fudge came from a show dog family in Birmingham and Toffee came from a farm near Middlewich, in Cheshire. Most of the time they got on well together although they could have the odd falling out as in any family and have to be kept apart for an hour or two. When they where two years old we took them to a pedigree dog near Bolton, called Branston. This gave us two litters of 'sweet and sour' puppies, five in each litter. The Kennel Club will only register six litters from any one bitch and we only had one litter a year from our girls although some people will breed two litters a year which we think is too much and would have worn the poor girls out before their time. Toffee lived to be fifteen years and twenty-two days while the average corgi lives to be about twelve.

CORGI STORIES.!!!!!!!!!!!

When you register pedigree dogs you have to have a kennel name, ours was Niktaw, well I tried everything else and they had already been used so I had to turn words backwards. Each puppy had to have two names of less than so many letters followed by Niktaw. Clare had great fun naming puppies, we had a whole litter of whisky's, Little Bell, Jack Daniels, Johnny Walker etc. On one occasion she named a puppy Hannibal Lector, the people who bought him called him Jack.

As Pembroke Corgis are so rare we sold them all over the country which meant that many of the buyers stayed as guests overnight when collecting their puppy. I would also email pictures of the puppies to their owners as they grew if they had chosen one before it was ready to leave its mother. I distinctly remember one young man staying to collect a puppy for his girlfriend who worked for the Northumberland hunt. He came through to the kitchen after breakfast and I opened the back door to go across the yard to the puppies in their pens. Toffee and Fudge shot out of the door, as per usual, and raced across the yard. He was amazed; he'd only seen fat Corgis waddling along behind old ladies before. He didn't know that they could run. We heard back from his girlfriend who told us that her Corgi followed the hunt with her on horse back. We sold Corgis literally to all ends of the country. One went up to Princess Street in Edinburgh and one down to London, one that we sent to Norfolk chewed up the arms of a Rolls Royce car! The owner rang to ask my advice, did I think that puppy classes would help. I said yes, they are called puppy classes but really they are owner classes. Corgis need a firm hand and this puppy wasn't getting that from its owner.

We took one puppy up to Pontefract to stay with Jennifer until her owner could collect her. Jenny's sister in law was staying at the time and, while playing with the puppy on the lawn she ran around the pond, but the puppy didn't! She was rather worried as the poor puppy was wet and shaking and it wasn't hers and she needed to get it dry before Jenny came home from work and the owner came to collect it. The puppy came to no harm for its experience.

The overseas manager of Coutts Bank came to collect his in a gold coloured Rolls Royce and asked if we had any bale string to use as a lead in case the puppy needed to have a run on the way back home. I remember him and his wife sitting in the play area and envying our view. She contacted me a few months later and asked me to buy the Times newspaper as her and the puppy had their picture in it. It was part of their advert for the French Chateaux they were selling.

Through the website a Japanese TV company contacted us as they were doing a programme on Royal dogs and they wanted to film a section on Corgi's. They came to see the farm and we took the corgis up the fields to show the crew how the dogs rounded up the cattle. In the end they didn't use our Corgi's in their programme as when they panned the cameras around the field they kept getting the local houses in on the shots and they just wanted country scenes and so they used a farm in Mid Wales for the programme, but it was an interesting experience.

CHAPTER 9
THE JOB

My part in this occupation was to provide everything that the guests needed as seamlessly as possible. This altered considerably over the years. In 1975, when I started I just had to put a sign at the bottom of the road and tidy a room up to the standard I would have expected to find when sleeping away. As tea facilities came into fashion I put a kettle and all the necessary extras into the utility room. When I joined the Welsh Tourist Board I found a whole list of rules to comply with. The tea facilities became standard in the bedrooms which the tourist board wanted to include, cups, saucers and teapots. Later I changed mine to mugs as it was what the customer wanted. I have now even stayed at hotels where you get mugs at breakfast time, which I understand as some of the workmen don't know how to put a cup on a saucer. Experience showed me that when the saucers were not used the table cloths were stained which gave me more work. Ensuite rooms started to become popular and so when we altered the house, the middle first, we started to put washbasins into bedrooms and later add ensuite bathrooms where it was possible. If you build from new you can plan these things from the word go but with an old house like ours it all took some planning. When Clare went to college we converted her room into a bathroom and knocked a hole in the wall through from one of the bedrooms. She came home feeling she wasn't wanted and commented that her head had slept were the toilet seat was. On the food front a farmhouse breakfast is still a farmhouse fry up but guests now expect more choice of cereals and fruits etc. After trying bread made in my sister's bread maker I invested in a machine and from that point on I gave guests home made bread. I made over twenty-five pounds of jam every year the favourites being Strawberry, Raspberry and Rhubarb and Blackberry and Apple. I would even sell the odd pot of jam to guests to take home. When the workers came in I put a toaster into the dinning room as I wouldn't cook before 7am and most people where happy with cereal and toast early in the morning. John would put the milk out when he got up to milk the cows at about six in the morning. I also added a chill cabinet with cold drinks and chocolates and an honesty box. I didn't want to go down the route of getting a drinks license as we felt that people would want to sit up later and we needed to be up in the morning. This led to the addition of a small freezer and microwave so that people could get something to eat if they really didn't want to go out again after booking in. The pub had stopped making meals at one time. Regulars would just buy their favourite meals and heat them up in the microwave and use the plastic plates and cutlery I provided or even bring in their own meals.

When I started doing evening meals in the mid 1970's I cooked good plain 'farmhouse' food, I felt that if people booked to stay on a farm that is what they would want. If I had enough guests in I would sometimes give a choice of sweet, but this was used by some guest to get two helpings. On one occasion the lemon meringue pie came back with the meringue eaten with, 'we don't like this can we have the apple pie please' the remains of the lemon meringue then had to be thrown away and so they had had two sweets. One of the favourite soups was my onions soup, a simple recipe using lots of onion and two Oxo cubes, cooked in seven minutes in the pressure cooker. I loved my pressure cooker. I always cooked my steak and kidney in it in a morning so that the meat was cold to put into the pastry to stop the pastry bottom from going soggy. Steamed sponge puddings came in various forms, a variety of home made jams, chocolate, syrup, treacle and sultana the treacle being stirred into the mix not put in the bottom, as well as a sliced lemon at the bottom or stewed fruits of various kinds. Fruit pies where popular and I do remember on day having a choice of Apple or Peach but as I took the peach pie out of the oven it did a somersault and landed on the floor, I had to tell the guests that the Peach pie was off the menu. If I could get hold of fresh peaches at a reasonable price they made the best pies ever. I would go down to Prestatyn market late in the afternoon and buy a box of bruised peaches for nearly nothing, they were a fiddle to peel but worth the effort.

When Clare was born in 1986 I all but stopped doing evening meals on a regular basis as we still had the pub at the end of the road and I had the freezer and microwave for the guests to use. Most people where quite happy with this arrangement but I did have a nasty experience with an Irish man who was with his wife and two babies. He wasn't happy that I couldn't provide a meal for the four of them off pat late in the evening. There was only John and I at home by that time and I didn't have anything in the fridge that I could magic into four extra meals. He was a bully of a man and he yelled at me for quarter of an hour. The more he yelled the more I dug my heels in, I wasn't going to be treated like that. He said that what was in the guest's freezer wasn't good enough for his family and that he wasn't taking them out again at eight o'clock at night that I must make them a meal. The next morning after breakfast I saw the wife and children outside in the play area and he came to pay and wouldn't pay the full amount as he said that the room was dirty and I was to go up to the room where he would show me. I didn't want to go upstairs with him and I just stood and told him there was nothing wrong with the room. After another thirty minutes of this I fetched John but he still refused to pay the full amount and in the end we accepted less to get rid of him. The family had been booked in for two nights and so I knew they would need to find accommodation between Greenhill and Holyhead so I rang every Tourist Information Centre along the route and warned them.

As time went on we started to receive enquiries from vegetarians. I found this a difficult one as we produce meat as a by product of the milk industry. Most of the calves born to a milking cow went for beef and, as we didn't have a big milk quote, we often kept these calves on to rear for beef for ourselves and to sell. I was even asked to provide a ‘vegetarian’ fry up on more that one occasion for this I used eggs, tomatoes, mushrooms and courgettes. On one occasion a prospective Welsh Nationalist Member of Parliament booked in during the run up to an election. He had booked in with us as the next day he had a photo shoot and interview taking place in the neighbouring farm. He came down for breakfast and ordered a vegetarian fry up; I bet that didn’t make the papers and he didn’t win the local seat.

On weekend of the funeral of Lady Diana, Princess of Wales we had two ladies booking in amongst others. I was full that weekend. One of the pair was particularly loud mouthed and so we could hear every word of what she was saying in the dining room from the kitchen. Now I’m a big royalist, our daughter, Jennifer, was lucky enough, with her dance club, to dance in Holywell Leisure Centre for Lady Diana and, as her mother, I had been honoured to watch the dancing. She had spoken to all the dancers individually after their performance. This was a very special memory for Jennifer. The kitchen TV was on as I had no intention of missing a minute of the funeral proceedings. This lady proudly announced that they had come out of London that weekend to get away from the fuss around the funeral as she was not a royalist. The sound on the TV went up in response to this and continued to go up the more fuss she made. When I got around to taking her breakfast order she proudly announced that she was vegetarian, why do they do that, I don't go around boasting I'm a meat eater. She ordered a vegetarian fry up which I served up to her after cooking it in lard, my revenge. She congratulated me on my fry up saying it was the best she'd ever had. I never had a complaint about my vegetarian fry ups even when they were cooked in lard.

A man booked himself and his nine-year-old son in on the internet for a two night stay on the farm so that his son could see where milk came from. I accepted the booking and took the deposit. A week before he arrived he emailed to make sure I had vegetarian sausages and burgers on the menu for breakfast. I very politely replied that I didn't serve up any imitation food. That all my food was local or home-made, local meats and eggs, home made bread and jam, butter not margarine. I got a very rude reply back telling me I should serve whatever the guests wanted. The tone of this email wasn't very nice and so I politely replied that I really didn't know why he wanted to stay on a farm which produced milk and beef if he was so against meat. He cancelled his stay saying that he wouldn't stay anywhere that animals were killed. No animals are killed on farms; they all go to abattoirs to be humanely killed.

I do find the attitude of some vegetarians difficult to understand, I did know a teenager who was vegetarian, but she didn't like vegetables, she lived on breakfast cereals and Linda McCartney meals. Many seem to have stopped eating meat deeming it cruel, without really looking into the subject. Over twenty species of UK animals are now extinct because no one eats them. Vegans I refused to take bookings from, they were the ultimate insult, not to even drink milk and want to stay on a milk farm. I did take vegetarian guests as, if they were silly enough to stay on a farm which reared beef cattle I would take their money off them.

Part of 'The Job' was to answer peoples enquires correctly, take their deposits and reply to them giving them all the information they had asked for. What it didn't include was mind reading but it came with the job. Some of the letters I would receive would need a mind reader to understand them and some were down right rude. I received a sheet of A4 with no address on it, the entire letter said and I quote: '£5 cheque enclosed as deposit for 1 en-suite room for two adults on 18th and 19th of this month. With regards, M. Hollies,' this was written in very scrawny biro. Another reply from a private guest was written on a company slip with the company's details crossed out. I was expected to write in a clear easily understood manner on my own headed paper, preferably typed for ease of reading mainly because I am slightly dyslexic and the computer has a spell check. This was clearly stated in the Welsh Tourist Board literature. Another way in which customers could be rude was by not turning up at all in which case I had lost my income and couldn't take in other bookings in case they came late. Sometime I would get a cancelation phone call when it was too late to rebook and on one occasion this was to say they got lost so stayed somewhere else. The advent of credit card machines put a stop to this as, if I had taken their card number, I could charge them the deposit and no one likes to lose money.

I must have passed the test with one particular guest as he was a hotel manager who stayed with us for a while. He had accepted the job of Hotel Manager at the Gateway to Wales Hotel at Sealand in Flintshire. As part of his package he was to have his own private accommodation outside the hotel, a flat in the local area, but when he arrived it wasn't ready and his employer wanted him to stay in a guest room. He was a mature gentleman and had had this experience before and he said No he would find accommodation until his flat was ready so that he wouldn't be on call 24 hours a day. After checking out accommodation providers in the area he booked in to stay with us in March 2000. When his flat was ready and he left he wrote in our guest book:

'*Thank you. I really enjoyed my stay at the farm. Very comfortable, welcoming, clean and great breakfast. Please call in and see me at the Gateway.*'

which we did. It was so sad that the hotel burnt down in 2017, this was well after he had moved on to other things.

Making sure that the guest rooms where secure and safe was part of my job. To my knowledge all my guests were trustworthy, and I rarely had a problem. Sachets would go missing sometimes but people had paid for them and expected to keep them. Also small bars of soap but I got round this by putting full size bottles in the rooms which is the norm in most hotels now. One day a single man asked me if I had a safe which we did have. Back in the late 1970's all our business was done in cash and we had had a floor safe concreted in when we renewed the middle downstairs room's floor. He showed me a wedge of cash and asked me to put it in the safe for the night. I didn't know how much cash there was and didn't want to be blamed if he thought any went missing and so I put it in an envelope, sealed the envelope and asked him to sign across the seal, that way we both knew if it had been tampered with. If he felt the room wasn't safe he obviously didn't trust people. I gave him his envelope back the next morning and he went away a happy man.

Another single gentleman left not so happy. He was a target shooter on his way to a competition. Apparently, he had a book in which he wrote notes about his shooting and the book went missing. He searched everywhere, in the room and in his car but it didn't turn up. We never did find it in the house, maybe he had left it at home.

A strange 'job' I was asked to do one day was to remove a butterfly from a bedroom. A young lady knocked on the office door not long after I had shown her to her room. She told me that there was a butterfly in the room. I must have looked confused as a nature lover I loved them. She went on to explain that she was scared of butterflies and so I had to go up and catch the poor thing which, by now had flown down the back of the bed head. It took me some time to catch it without hurting it. I've heard of people who are scared of spiders, I'm none too keen on them myself, but butterflies was a first in my book.

On more than one occasion guests have locked themselves out of their cars, usually Americans using hired cars. As nine times out of ten we couldn't help them they would call the AA out to solve the problem. They would then have to wait for the AA to arrive, all the time trying to come up with solutions to the problem. Although we could do nothing this did waste us a lot of time, hanging around reassuring guests while we all waited.

Waiting for guests to book in can be a time-consuming job. After I had to wait up until one in the morning for a guest who wasn't in the least apologetic I changed all my adverts etc to say that the booking in time was ten in the evening. As few people read past the first couple of lines of any literature this didn't always work, this was one of the problems of the job.

I remember asking a guest what time they were booking in to be told between two and three in the afternoon. I then had to pay someone to come in after lunch to house sit and wait for these guests as we were going out. As we drove down the road at ten in the morning a strange car was driving up. I thought it could be the guests but we were in a rush so we didn't stop. We got back home at about five in the afternoon to start milking and our house sitter was still sat, the guests hadn't booked in. When they eventually did book in late in the evening I asked if they had arrived earlier and they said yes. I had paid the house sitter for nothing.

I've even had guests try and book in before nine in a morning, while the guests in the room they had booked were still eating breakfast. I had to politely ask them to wait in the sitting room for a couple of hours which they were pleased to do as it turned out. There's nout as queer as folk. We often had to pay someone to house sit so that we could go out, otherwise we wouldn't had had a life of our own which I think everyone is entitled to.

Cleaning was an obvious part of the job, greatly helped by Claire and Gwyneth and for a short while, Louise who popped in now and then to give me a hand, over the years however one job did annoy me intensely. To blend in with the oak beams all my dining tables and chairs where black Priory furniture. Proper wood, none of this melamine stuff. As time went on it was very noticeable that people didn't realise that proper wood marks when boiling hot tea and coffee pots and hot water jugs are put directly on the wood. This is why my tables were always set with place mats and mats for the tea and coffee pots. I couldn't believe the number of times people would put the pots straight onto the table when the mats were in front of them. They had just picked the pots up off the mats why couldn't they put them back on the mats. The work involved in getting these white marks off the tables was quite onerous. I had to buy special cream to lift the marks and follow that with a complete re-wax of the table and then a good polish.

Bed making was another big part of the job which, on your own, can take up a lot of time but with two of you chatting away at the same time it can soon be done. I've seen hotels where they only use one bed maker per floor and it must be a slow, lonely job. Susan and I became the fastest bed makers in the west. We originally had blankets in all the rooms until duvets became fashionable. We had to keep both for a while as some older customers would demand blankets being creatures of habit. We also needed a choice of both feather and foam pillows for people with alleges to feather pillows or a preference for feather pillows. Duvets can be a problem to change if you don't have a plan of action. Here's a tip: When you peel off a duvet cover leave it inside out, wash it and iron it inside out. When it needs to be put back on the bed each of you run a hand down the inside of the seam until you get to the corner and grab hold of it. Then grab hold of the end of the duvet with the same hand and just turn the cover over back onto the duvet. Job done. When you have changed as many beds as we have you need to do it efficiently as the saying goes; 'Time is money'. After all the children had left home and the milking cows had gone down the road I even got John well trained at bed making.

We also often had to provide a cot for babies. Susan and Jennifer had used the cot which was originally bought for me in 1949 which was a 'utility' cot. Utility furniture was made and sold during and just after the war and it was solid basic furniture. This cot was wonderful for storing and bringing out at short notice for guests. For storage you lifted out the mattress and the base and the four sides swivelled to lie flat against the wall. It was on casters so you could roll it up and down the landing without a struggle. When Clare was born and I needed another cot I borrowed one from my cousin but one night when the cot was already in use we had a late booking for an Italian family who needed a cot and so we had to take Clare's cot down and move it to a guest room and she had to sleep in her pram. That night I think we had more children than adults in the house.

I have also been asked to provide adapter plug for overseas visitors who have 'forgotten' or 'lost' there plugs. I kept these in various sizes and shapes having to remember that the adapter plugs we use abroad are the wrong way round. I usually 'acquired' my stock from guest bedrooms when they had been left behind. Maps were another favourite thing for guests to leave and these could be recycled back to other guests. Travellers from Ireland would leave Irish Maps and those going over to Ireland would leave their British maps in the dust bins.

Later on flavoured teas were expected by some and so I had to keep a supply of various flavours in stock. One thing I refused to provide were sugar coated cereals. My children were never allowed to have them and if more sugar is needed on a cereal it can be added.

Who pays the bill? Well I had to be very diplomatic when this problem arose. It usually occurred when people were visiting family. Arguments could break out between the local and the visitor as to who was paying. I really didn't mind who paid as long as someone did.

The window cleaner could cause me a problem as he usually arrived up first thing in a morning. He was booked to come once a month, it saved us an extra job and wasn't expensive. If I had a full house I had to tell him which windows he could clean first so that no embarrassing situations occurred. As far as I know we did manage to avoid any difficult moments.

Keeping guests healthy is a strange problem. When the children were younger they would always catch the latest infectious illnesses just as the summer holiday bookings came in and I would try and keep them away from guests children. I was doing very well at this one summer when they had chickenpox until I came in from the fields to find a neighbour's child playing with Susan and Jennifer. I sent her home immediately, but it wasn't soon enough. A few days later she went on holiday with her family to a Butlins holiday camp. By the end of the week all the children in Butlins had chickenpox. If guests found out our children had a problem most of them were quite happy and would say 'don't worry our children need to catch it and get it over with'.

Keeping guest happy is the most important job which I worked very hard to accomplish in various ways. Keeping my children happy at the same time kept me extremely busy but occasionally guest would ask if they could take my children with them on their days out which was good for all of us. Mum and Dad were happy, children were happy and I was happy. Susan and Jennifer went for a day out to the sea side with a Dutch family one day and improved their education by learning the Dutch word for Spider, (spinnekop) which they found amusing. They also spent many an evening with the Dutch children playing Snap. Snap is easy in any language isn't it?

Clare was invited out with a paediatric doctor and his wife and daughter one day. She was about six years old at the time and used a booster cushion in the car. I went and fetched her booster cushion and strapped her into the back seat of their car but I was shocked to see that not only didn't their daughter have a booster cushion but they didn't even bother to put her seatbelt on. I worried about Clare all day but she did arrive home in one piece. Children are your most valuable possessions and you need to look after them properly and bring them up to be good adults.

CHAPTER 10
REGULARS.

When the customer base moved from primarily tourists to primarily business people I started to get regular customers. When I say regulars, this could mean once a year, once a month or even once in a new moon. Often, if there was a good contract in the area they would stay for four nights a week for a number of weeks. My ‘once every three months’ jewellery rep would ring and say, ‘Hello, it’s the good looking one speaking’. He wasn’t tall dark and handsome, no he was short blonde and middle-aged. He must have had a high opinion of himself although to tell the truth he was a very nice man from whom I bought a piece of jewellery for a gift on one of his visits. He needed to stay somewhere where he knew his car would be secure as it was full of valuable jewellery and had asked our local jeweller about accommodation in the area. Mr. & Mrs. Scott, the jewellers, were also milk customers and neighbours and so they recommended me.

One gentleman from Devon always rang and said, ‘I’m ringing long distance’. Given that I had bookings from all over the world this phrase always amused me. He was a retired gentleman from Suffolk who came up to visit family and he came from an era when a phone would have been a luxury, so I did understand why he said it. I often knew voices better than names and faces. When people rang up I knew straight away if I'd spoken to them before.

John Lakeman from Seven Oaks came twice a year to service and calibrate some machinery in a local factory. He came from September 1993 through to April 2003. He told us that he had had a heart attack in 2001 and so we assumed that he retired after that. One evening he arrived up after booking to find that he had forgotten his suitcase. Someone had rung him while he was packing his car and he'd put the tools in to service the machines, gone in the house to answer the phone, come out said goodbye to his wife and driven off. We had to provide him with a razor and other essential toiletries along with what was already in the rooms and he had to go M&S before work to buy underwear etc. After his stay I bought small baskets for all the rooms and put in them razors, nail files, hair clips and plasters. The rooms already had soap, shampoo, shower caps etc. These are just little things, but they added to the comfort and feeling of well being for guests.

We had a regular customer who once left his toothbrush behind after one stay. He rang me and asked me to keep it until his next visit. I'm afraid he then became Alistair Toothbrush to us. We did use nicknames for some people which was fine unless they found out.

On the milk round we had a lady who, at one time, came out every morning to tell us the continuing saga of the mouse in the kitchen, were it had been and what it had eaten. She lived in a council house and eventually the council workers found a nest in the grill of her gas cooker. Susan and Jennifer were quite young at the time and christened her 'the mouse lady'. They did manage to call her that to her face once, so embarrassing all round.

Miss Higgins came twice a year starting in May 1993 through until 2003. She was a retired teacher from Newcastle. She travelled to Ireland for two weeks every year to visit family. She stayed with me the night before her ferry over from Holyhead and again when the ferry landed back in the UK. Every year she would arrive up in the same hand knitted woolly hat and the same navy-blue anorak but in a brand new. She would write to me to confirm her booking giving me a list of her dietary requirements. After settling her into her room she would come down and ring the bell to ask if she could use the tea facilities in the room and have a bath. Her first visits where at the time of shared bathrooms. About 5am the following morning she would have her bath. She would run off every ounce of hot water and leave a ring around the top of the bath tub. I'm sure that if she moved the water would have run over the top of the bath onto the floor. When she came down to breakfast she would bring two huge flasks and ask me to fill one with black tea and one with milky coffee. She would then order a full cooked breakfast and toast. She would fetch a glass bottle out of her handbag and fill it with milk from the jug on the table to go with the black tea and butter all the toast in the rack, fold it into a napkin and put that in her bag with the bottle of milk. After she had left I would go up to her room to find that she had taken all the sachets, tea coffee sugar chocolate, and anything else she thought was for taking. I didn't make a penny in profit from this customer. Once I had got use to her routine I would limit the number of sachets in her room and warn the other customers to watch her at the breakfast table. I let her stay for the amusement value she gave to the other guests who would have a quiet titter as they watched her.

In May 1996 Jennifer got married and I let her stay the night before the wedding, I had closed that week as we where busy preparing for the big day which was on a Thursday, Jennifer's birthday. I showed her the wedding cake I had made for Jennifer and Gareth, three tiers with a bride and groom on the top and icing sugar imitation bouquets on the other tiers. One year I really was unable to take her on her outward journey to Ireland and so I recommended another guest house. She can't have been happy as, on her way home, she arrived up to see if I had any vacancies. One year she couldn't unlock the petrol cap on her car and so Jennifer's husband, Gareth, opened it for her. She refused to drive down to the garage with it unlocked and so she made him go down with her and open it again at the garage. When Gareth couldn't get it to lock after she'd filled it with petrol she rang the AA to come and sort it out for her. She obviously thought the world of her car. A few years before we retired she stopped coming and I presume, as she was retired when we first met her, that she had died.

Another set of 'regulars' during 1998 and 1999 who were not going to work but were looking at canal boats to buy. There was a company in Flint called Hallmark who made canal boats and people from all over the country would come up to see the boats and, maybe, buy one, mainly to live on. Retiring to a canal boat became quite popular; the freedom to travel around the country staying in your own bed at night was appealing. I had so many customers from this business that when Christmas came along I made them a Canal Boat Christmas cake. It sat in the icing sugar water, moored up to the bank with platted silk 'ropes' onto chocolate posts made from various chocolates and Father Christmas was coming out of the boat chimney. I took it down to them with some of my brochures and they rewrote their advertising to state that if the guests bought a boat and had stayed with me the company would pay their accommodation bill. This contract went on for quite a while but I think the company went out of business in the end when recession hit everyone.

One year we had a team of guest up from the south coast for a week, they had been contracted to change all the signs on every Santander building society in the country.

They had booked an evening meal at about the time we had put a full beef in the freezer. We used to have our own beef killed so that we knew what we were eating. These guests enjoyed the beef so much on their last day they came back after work and bought frozen beef from me to take home. A few months later a milk customer had been on holiday on the south coast and gone into Marks and Spencer's. The lady in M&S, who served them asked were they where from and told them that her husband had been in Holywell and taken home some wonderful beef. It's a small world.

There are some strange jobs about! One year we had a gang of six men from near Crieff in Scotland for a week. They were taking down and replacing the barbed wire on the huge electricity pylons. They went all around the country doing this job. They ranged from the boss down to the young teenager who hadn't been away from home before. After dinner on the second night they told me they were going to walk up to Holywell for a drink in one of the local pubs. After having a drink or two they decided to have some fun with the young lad and so when he went to the toilet they sneaked off without him. They came back and put themselves to bed. Well eventually he found his way back but he didn't have a key, his work mates had locked him out. He went around to the back of the house and, as luck would have it, he found a ladder leaning along the bottom of the wall, left there after a job not finished. So far so good, he could put the ladder up to his friend's window and wake them to let him in. This is where it all went terribly wrong for him, he got the wrong window. He chose our bedroom window. He climbed up the ladder and knocked on the window which naturally woke us up. Now we sleep naked. We woke up and looked at each other in surprise; we had never had anyone knocking on our bedroom window in the night before. I jumped out of bed, as my side was nearest the window, and very carefully, holding the curtain across my body, peeped out. The poor boy nearly fell of the ladder with shock at seeing me, never mind my shock at seeing someone there. He told us his problem and John put some cloths on and went down stairs to let him in. The next morning at breakfast there was a deadly hush around their breakfast table. They really didn't know how I was going to react at all. My feeling was that boys will be boys and no harm was done but I thought I'd just get my own back in a small way. I walked into the dinning room and looked at them; they looked back at me in trepidation. I said 'it's a long time since I'd had a young man try and climb in through my bedroom window'. The poor boy blushed but it broke the ice and after a good laugh, we carried on. It's no good worrying about a small mistake is it now.

A company called Kingspan opened in Greenfield and contractors working there stayed with us from 1994. One of the contract from this company was with Dave Bumbry and his team from near Scarborough who stayed with us on and off until 2005. They were a happy gang of men from 'Heartbeat' country in the north east, one of them lived in a cottage next to the station that the TV programme used to film from. It all started one November afternoon, when Clare was only about two or three years old and playing on the kitchen floor with her toys while I was cooking, I got a knock on the back door. There was a tall, good looking, suited and booted middle aged gentleman standing there. He wanted to see my accommodation. Well I had to bring him in and walk him over the top of Clare's toys through to the guest's side of the house. He explained what he wanted but I thought I wouldn't get the contract after he saw the kitchen with toys all over the floor. This was the first time I had met Dave Bumbry and once he had introduced himself he explained that his team were staying in a hotel in Holywell but the team were threatening to go home because the food was so bad- small helping badly cooked, and asked could I take them the next night before he had a full scale riot on his hands. It was hard work, they wanted a full cooked breakfast on the table by 7am every morning and a three-course dinner on the table at 7pm every night as they where working twelve hours shifts to get the job done. They were one of the few group's people I did regular evening meals for after Clare was born but they were such a happy crowd. They would come in for dinner with bottles of wine and always fill me a glass. They ate everything I put in front of them every night. The only problem was that when they fitted a machine they stayed until the job was finished, I think the longest stay was seven men for ten days. Dave, himself was partial to my homemade Christmas pudding, I had served this up one night as I had a spare one over from Christmas and he would ask for it so I had to make more. Twice I had put Xmas pudding down on the menu for them and on those evenings he had to go and eat out with the bosses of Kingspan, he was so disappointed. Dave and the team worked hard and one evening poor Dave fell asleep on the sofa in the guest's front room so I took a picture of him and sent it back to his office where they printed it out and put it on the wall, poor Dave, they said they now knew what he did when he was away. It was a measure of the rapport we had that I felt able to do that. The company that Dave and his team worked for, Kingspan, also had other factories including one on the border between northern and southern Ireland. They told me that in 1991 they were travelling back on the ferry in their white van when they were pulled over by customs for a routine search. Some time, later the IRA tried to bomb the Prime Ministers official home at10 Downing Street in London, from a white van; Dave was contacted by customs and quizzed over the white van parked behind them, and its passengers as that was the one with the bomb in it. Kingspan went on to buy factories abroad and Dave and his team told us that they were now travelling overseas to fit the machines and so we didn't see them after 2005.

During July and August of 2005, for eight weeks, we had a young girl called Irene from Singapore staying while she worked in Warwick Chemicals in Mostyn during her holiday while in university. Her parents had sent her to boarding school in the UK at the age of 10 to give her a good education. It was at the time that Singapore was given back to China and many people she knew where leaving the country. She was doing a Doctorate in Chemistry in St. Mary's University in London and had a scholarship in Warwick Chemicals in Mostyn a few miles along the coast. She was a quiet girl and we took her out with us on a number of occasions to see the countryside as she had no transport. She was taken to work each day by a local who worked in Warwick and passed our road on their way. We often wonder where youngsters like that are today.

Our resident 'wood carver', Eliot, stayed with us to work on some carvings in the Greenfield Valley our local Heritage Park, in 2003 and 2004. He had a wonderful artistic flair for working with wood and did more than one piece of work in the Valley. He would arrive up with his guitar and, if his partner came with him he would ask if it was OK to light candles in the room. I suppose if you saw him you might call him a hippy but he certainly knew his job.

John Redman was another regular and although he didn't stay more than two or three days at a time he came quite often during 2005, through to 2010, sometimes with an associate. He was inventing a machine using EEC grant aid, to better dredge the river Dee. Now, believe it or not, most grains of sand are irregular in shape but the grains in the Dee Estuary are spherical and when you move them up hill they just roll down again. It's amazing what you learn when you run a guest house. Some days he would come back very frustrated when the sand wouldn't stay put.

British Aerospace worked with a factory in Toulouse in France the consortium was put together using EU monies. British Aerospace made the wings which were either flown or shipped out to Toulouse where the planes were finished. Some British workers working in Toulouse all week flew out from Broughton Airport on Monday morning and returned on Friday night. Danny Sewell, originally from Mold, worked for British Aerospace in Toulouse, and became a regular guest. He had divorced from his wife and so had moved to Toulouse and eventually married a French girl, they had a young daughter. They came to stay for a number of years, arriving in 2002 and staying for a week or two during the summer months for about five years. I used to have great fun with their little girl, she had numerous teddy bears on her bed and so I would move the teddy bears around the room, they would sit on top of the wardrobe or on the curtain pelmets or anywhere else I could think of. She enjoyed coming back in an evening to see were they where. They got in touch with Danny's children from his first marriage after a break of several years which made them all happy. This was another family who always had the same bedroom, a home from home. One summer they said that they where glad to get over to the UK as it was so hot in Toulouse they had had to buy a plastic swimming pool for the garden to sit in each evening to cool down and that the land was parched.

Roger Wicking stayed with us with his daughters, Lorna and Lorraine. He was divorced and would come up from London for the weekend once a month to see them and they would all stay with us. Lorna was a natural on the farm and loved to help outside with her father. We are still 'friends' on Facebook and she did her year out from university in Australia working on all sorts of farms and even helped a llama to give birth. She visited us when she got home and showed us her key ring with a preserved baby crocodile head on it. The baby had bitten her and, and as crocodiles are very susceptible to infections, it had died and the manager had had it preserved and gave it to her on the key ring as a farewell gift. He had even offered her a permanent job as she was so good with the crocodiles but she chose to come back to the UK. Roger, on occasions, brought his girlfriend, Diane with him. When they got married we were invited and so drove down to London for the wedding and reception in a village hall on the outskirts of London. It had the last tube station outside of London to make it easy for London friends and country friends to get to. It's the first time I've been to a wedding where the groom did the washing up! It was also 'Grand National' day and we never missed watching the race. My great grandfather had trained the 1928 Grand Nation winner, Tipperary Tim, a hundred to one outsider. It still holds the record for the least number of horses to finish with only two left standing. The jockey was a solicitor from Chester, his friends had said to him: 'You will stand a chance if they all fall' and they did. At the wedding, in a back room of the village hall someone found a TV but when we switched it on the reception was so bad we could only see lines. Someone else went to the kitchen and came back with a tin foil dish which he screwed up and pushed into the aerial hole on the back of the TV. It worked perfectly and about a dozen of us who were interested got to watch the race. This is the only race we put a bet on for old time's sake. My great grandfather, Joseph Dodd, had pulled himself up by his boot laces after running away from home age twelve to work with horses for Lord Dudley and he had a very interesting life running up to becoming a Grand National winning trainer.

Roger wasn't the only father to visit his children. Another gentleman, Mr Goodall, visited his son on and off for over two years from 1997. The son had elephantitus and had to have regular medical check ups to watch his health. I always felt bad taking money from people visiting like this; it wasn't easy to see children split from caring parents.

Another father fetched his son up, on a weekend when he had custody, to visit friends locally. These friends booked him in for two nights. When he arrived he told me he wanted to walk his son up Snowdon. The next morning they didn't come down for breakfast until 10a.m and they were not rushing to leave. I felt it safer to explain to him that it could take him five or six hour's to walk up and down Snowdon and that Snowdon was an hours drive away from the farm. Thankfully he decided against trying the walk. This gentleman left without paying. This is something I didn't have happen very often but I have always gone to great lengths to get my money back. After visiting his friends to get his address and phone number I eventually had to threaten him with the small claims court. As he now knew my phone number he wouldn't answer his phone to me. As luck would have it John had a visit from the police to check his gun licence and see that the gun was well locked up and safely stored. This was done regularly every five years. I told the police man about this customer and so he rang the man using his mobile phone. As this was a different phone number he answered and, I expect, got quite a shock when the policeman identified himself and asked him to pay. That did the trick, a cheque arrived through the post and it didn't bounce.

The first time I had a 'none payer' I never did get my money, it only happened once. On the second time the bill was to be paid by a local company which, unbeknown to me, had become bankrupt. I drove down to the factory and parked my car across the gateway and stopped anyone entering or leaving. They paid me out of the petty cash.

Another set of 'regulars' started to arrive in 2007 for the 'Speed Awareness Course' which was held in Greenfield Business Park. There were different people each weekend all shaking in their boots with fear as to what was going to happen to them but preferring the course to having points on their licences. The Chief Constable for North Wales at that time was Mr. Bunston. He became famous for his love of speed cameras, many of our guests were caught while on holiday, unaware of the number of cameras in the area. I added up and found I had taken over £2,000 in money just from people doing the Speed Awareness Course over two years. The favourite quote was 'I've never had points on my license in all the years I've been driving and I'm not starting now'. If you lived in North Wales speeding fines where a fact of life which you took in your stride, especially if you had to drive a lot as part of your job.

One elderly lady booked and said she would arrive by train in the early afternoon as she didn't want to drive so far. Well early afternoon came and went and eventually she arrived about 8pm. The poor dear had bought her train ticket to Greenfield. Well the Greenfield railway station near Holywell closed in the 1960's; you have to get off at either Flint or Prestatyn now. She got to Manchester to change for Greenfield, near

Oldham, but luckily someone on the station realised where she really wanted to go and she had to get another train down to Flint. She was in her 80s and so very tired and flustered by the time she got to me. Many of these ‘customers’ were elderly, not what you would call real speed guys, often they where ‘caught’ doing about 33 or 34 miles per hour.

As well as the Speed Awareness course there were courses for people who had had minor accidents. The police would decide that the offence was better treated by putting the driver on a refresher course that by taking them to court. On these courses part of the course was for three ‘customers’ to go out with the instructor in his car and to drive for him to see the quality of their driving. One of our customers on this course came back to tell us that, when she was sitting in the back of the car an elderly gentleman was driving and the instructor was in the front passenger seat, an ambulance was coming up behind them with his siren going and his blue lights on. The driver didn’t pull in and when the instructor asked him to he said ‘No the ambulance could wait’. The instructor asked him to pull over in a lay by and immediately took his license off him and made him ring his daughter to take him home. He banned him from driving on the spot.

A Mr & Mrs. Clough turned up for the driving course and were amazed that my dining room was covered in pictures relating to the 1928 Grand National winner, Tipperary Tim. This is because the horse was trained by my Great Grandfather, Joseph Dodd and, since the death of his youngest daughter our generation had been to the auction to buy back the memorabilia as his daughter specified in her will that it had to be sold in auction. Mr. Clough was the youngest member of his family and only a very small baby when the race was won but the story in the family read like this. Every Grand National they put sixpence on the race, their only bet of the year, and his oldest brother had had the honour of picking the horse that year. He'd picked Tipperary Tim and his mother had spent the whole morning complaining about what she could have done with sixpence, it was a lot on money in 1928 and the horse was a 100/1 outsider, with a tube in its throat to help it to breath. Well he won the race and they won the equivalent of two weeks wages. He wasn't the only guest with a link to Tipperary Tim.

John Swallow lived on Saddleworth moor and travelled down to work in the Greenfield Business Centre every day. After a while he found this an onerous journey and so he would stay with us on either a Tuesday or Wednesday night to break up the week. He did this for about three years arriving in 2006 and only leaving when he retired to play golf. He would often leave something in his bedroom which I just saved for him until the following week. I often had some strange objects waiting to be collected. Odd socks were quite common.

Shawn had a market stall and he also travelled long distances to set up his stall in either Flint, Holywell or Mold markets and so sometimes he would travel down the night before and stay with us, parking his white van in the back yard and it was too big for the front.

The power station down at Connah's Quay proved a good source of 'regulars' as each part of it had to have annual checkups. I was a bit further away that some other bed and breakfasts and hotels but, when they where full, I would have men from the power stations staying with me for a week or two while they checked the plant over.

Another of our 'regulars' was a weather man; he worked for the metrological office in London. He travelled around the country twice a year to inspect all the unmanned weather stations. While with me he would check weather stations from Liverpool down to Mid Wales, the closest being at Hawarden near Chester. One year he gave Clare a 'weather mug'. It had a picture of the sun covered by a cloud on it but when you put hot liquid into it the sun came out and the cloud disappeared. Clare loved her mug, it was much preferable to the Tetley Tea Bags mug which played the Tetley advert tune when you picked it up, or even when you opened the dish washer door if it was waiting to be washed.

Mr. Pole checked lighthouses and buoys in the river Mersey and the river Dee. He worked for Trinity House in London and arrived twice a year starting in 2000 and staying biannually up to 2006. He had to go out at night with a pair of binoculars and make sure the lights worked on the buoys as well as making sure they hadn't come adrift and floated away.

Some of my regulars where so 'regular' that if they were coming in at a time that we would be out we had an arrangement by which a key would be left under a flowerpot outside the front door. There were lots of pots outside the front door and I had a row of hanging baskets and up to twelve big black or blue tubs of flowers along with smaller pots. The tubs were up to about two foot across and eighteen inches deep, for the younger generation this reads as up to 60 cm. across and 45 cm. deep. They had arrived at Greenhill filled with minerals mixed with treacle which we would put into the fields for the cattle to make sure they had all the minerals and vitamins they needed especially in the spring when the grass would grow too quickly and may be deficient in some vitamins and minerals. A cow with calcium or magnesium deficiency is a very sick animal and needs instant treatment or it will die. You had to get up close to an animal lying on its side, kicking and thrashing about like a mad thing and put a needle into a vein either in its neck or into the milk vein underneath leading to the udder. You then fixed a tube to this and a bottle of calcium or magnesium liquid which you had to hold in the air so that it ran into the cow while making sure that the needle didn't come out. Although it was possible to do this as a one-man job it wasn't advisable. It was difficult enough for two people to do. It was even better not to have the problem in the first place and so we would buy the tubs of vitamins and minerals. We then made these tubs into flower pots, John would drill holes in the bottom and I would plant them up. I had a set of black tubs full of spring daffodil bulbs to match the daffodils I had planted the whole way up the road, and a set of blue tubs full of geraniums for the summer months. I could drag the geranium tubs into the back shed for the winter so that the frost wouldn't kill them although; being so near the sea and only one hundred feet above sea level this wasn't a big problem. I did once keep them alive for four years outside. I had a hose pipe system set up and could water the tubs quite quickly, I often did this while waiting for guests to come down for breakfast as the tubs where under the dining room window and I could see when they came down to eat. I have always loved to garden as my father and grandmother before me. Al, one of our 'regulars' from USA, even has a video of me planting my broad beans in the spring. I would try and grew a lot of my own fruit and vegetables to serve to guests for their evening meals or to turn into jam for the breakfast table.

Have you heard about the company called Green Thumb? This was a franchise set up after a gentleman worked in America and saw a similar company there. The company will come and mow your lawn for you to save you the job; they do other things as well such as fertilizing the lawn and getting the moss out. The owner set up the company as a franchise which means that he didn't employ the staff, he sold people a package and a name and they found there own customers. He had a training office down in Deeside but some of his trainees stayed with me as I was cheaper than the big hotels close by the site, and more homely.

My last 'regular' before our retirement arrived in the spring of 2011 to do the electrical refit in, what was Woolworths in Holywell High Street and which is now Weatherspoons. Dave stayed four days a week for about a month, until his part of the work was completed.

CHAPTER 11
FOUR NIGHTS A WEEK

During 1992 and 1993 Kimberly Clark closed its factory in Kent and opened a new one in Flint, just down the road. At that time there were favourable grants for new companies moving into the area. Also at that time Greenfield had had planning permission for a new housing estate of over 200 houses abutting the farm land and a number of Kimberly Clark staff moved up to the area. The company paid these people's accommodation for a month to give them time to find new homes and to move. A number of men stayed at our B&B over that period for four nights a week, some moving in locally and some a bit further afield. A few of their wives became friends as they had children in Greenfield school with Clare.

A local company, Henrob, had got a big contract in 2000 to develop a way of riveting aluminium for the car industry. All the people working on this project were working on computers in the offices of the company and most of them came from Birmingham. This contract coincided with the big foot and mouth outbreak when they closed all public footpaths in the UK and ruined the tourism industry for a long time. What to do? We were lucky, the front of the house, where the guests parked, could be shut off from the farm at the back by means of a gate and none of these guests lived in the countryside or near a 'foot and mouth' area so we shut the back gate and the guests continued to arrive, driving over a carpet soaked in disinfectant. It was a good thing our guest house income was still available as the whole debacle almost ruined our farm income. We couldn't sell any animals at all and so the building where full of cattle as the cows continued to calve at regular intervals. Because we couldn't sell any of our old cows the 'somatic cell count' in the milk went up and we had our milk cheques penalised as our contract said we couldn't sell milk with a cell count over two hundred and fifty. It didn't matter that organic milk can be sold up to a thousand cells or that there was foot and mouth in the country preventing anyone moving animals. The somatic cell count counts the white blood cells in the milk; too many are a sign that there *may be* bacteria in the milk, a common sign of mastitis in the cows but also common in older cows. This is why it is rare for a dairy cow to be on a farm over five years old even though a cow can have a life span of up to twenty years. The dairy's had a field day and must have made a good profit from this bonus as the milk was still useable and our milk went to a cheese factory where the cell count didn't matter quite so much. The cell count is to prevent bugs in bottled milk although this is pasteurised and so no one was at any risk.

Andrew was one of our first Henrob customers and was the last to leave us sixteen months later but, at one point we had six men, four nights a week right through the foot and mouth period. It was a god send. Andrew was a lovely young man who had marriage problems, he eventually had a divorce from his first wife and married a local girl and now lives nearby. He introduced me to his second wife as his second mum. Although he was no trouble as a guest he did have one problem, his feet smelt. Whenever you walked into his bedroom you had to dash across to open the window and spray the room with air freshener. Andrew's bedroom was the nearest to ours, it was at the front of the house with a view across the water. It had been used by all our girls over the years, but when we realised that we were having so many single customers we asked Clare to move into the small room next to us. The blackmail was that she could have the room any way she wanted. We bought her new pine furniture and she chose yellow and red as the colour scheme. A few years later when she went away to college we decided we could make the small room into an ensuite bathroom for the room that became Andrew's. We rang our joiner to give him plenty of notice, thinking he would be busy but he wasn't and he turned up to start two weeks later which didn't amuse Clare, she felt as if we didn't love her any more. He knocked through the wall and put in a bathroom suit. The toilet was just where Clare's head used to be when she was in bed. When we were revamping these rooms I happened to go to a car boot sale and saw some Sara Moon pictures, these were from the 1960's but I liked them and hung them up in this room. Over the next couple of years I managed to find some more and soon had a good display around the room, about six in all. John and Clare didn't approve, they said the pictures where spooky, if they where it fit in with the character of the house as you will read later on in the Baldrick chapter.

Poltec were another company we worked with for a while during 2007 and 2008. They did training courses in the Greenfield Business centre and we often had people to stay for the week on a course. This company were slightly different as they paid the bill not the person staying. This varied from company to company. I did have a Norwegian company who had booked in some staff the boss arrived from his more expensive hotel up the road to pay the bill on a Sunday morning. The bill was for over a thousand pounds and his credit card bounced, he had gone over its limit. He was mortified and had to pay me on his private card as he couldn't sort out the problem until the Monday morning.

The Tourist Board inspectors told us to theme our rooms. In the next room along I had hung a seascape which I'd bought in a house sale in Holywell, the view being of the sea with a beach etc. and so I thought that was appropriate. Over the years this picture faded and was changed but it had a good oak frame so I kept it. Many years later on the run up to the Grand National there was a write up in the Shropshire Star about our family and our connection to the Grand National. I wanted to frame it and add it to the Tipperary Tim memorabilia in the Dining Room so out came the oak frame with the seascape. I opened up the back and under the seascape there was a certificate presented to someone for their donation to the Methodist Church. I 'Googled' this and found out that between 1898 and 1908 a collection was made to build a Methodist Hall in the City of Westminster. People were asked to donate a guinea towards building it and they all given a certificate. There are fifty books in the Methodist Hall listing all the names of the donators. I emailed them and told them what I'd found and asked if they wanted it. They told me that they only had eleven certificates and had a display of them on the wall with the certificates and an explanation of how they had been found. My certificate was added to the wall although I have never been down to London to see it.

Indi was another member of the Henrob team; he was a lovely Indian gentleman with a wife who had expensive tastes! I remember him telling me she was off on holiday to Dubai with her sister and, because gold was so much cheaper over there, she intended to buy herself some more jewellery. He was very worried as to how much she was going to spend. We had more in common with Indi that any other of these contractors. He had been brought up in India on the family farm and had used some of the same machinery as we had in our childhood. A turnip chopper machine was one of these as it was always the children's job to turn the handle as the turnips where put into the top to be cut down to chippings to make them easier for the animals to digest. Some things don't change whichever side of the world you live in, it wouldn't be long before your arms where aching but you had to keep going or you got shouted at.

As these guests were staying before and after Christmas, if I was baking I would leave mince pies and other treats out on a plate for them when they got back from work. One day Indi arrived with some Indian treats for us to try. I always tried to make contract workers feel at home because they were away from home so much. I would try and make sure that they had the same bedroom every week so that it felt like home from home. In the guests sitting room/hall I had a chill cabinet, small freezer and microwave. I sold cold drinks, chocolates and crisps and kept some ready meals in the freezer to be heated in the microwave. If it was a cold, dark, wet evening customers wouldn't always want to go back out to eat. Some of the regulars would buy their own ready meals to heat up for dinner. I tried my hardest to keep my customers happy and feeling at home.

Paul Bell who was working down at Mostyn docks, was from Morecambe. He was the site manager for the company who extended the docks when P&O Ferries said they would dock there as Liverpool Docks had put up the docking fees. He was with us four days a week for fourteen months, arriving in May 2001. His hobby was model railways which, he told us, filled his attic. Just occasionally, if there was a problem, he would need to stay a fifth night. On one occasion, in the October, Clare had been abroad on a school trip and was due back on the Friday night. During the afternoon Paul rang to ask if he could stay another night. His room had already been cleaned and I had a full house booked so, to keep him happy, I told him he could have Clare's room. Poor Clare arrived home late that night after a sixteen hour bus journey to find she was sleeping on a 'put you up' in the front room. She said she felt unwanted yet again. P&O didn't use Mostyn docks for long in the end, but did run some ferries in during December of 2001, later they went back to Liverpool but the docks are in regular use by the people building the wind farms out in the Irish Seas and by British Aerospace who ship the plane wings down to Mostyn to be loaded onto boats to take to Toulouse in France to put on the body of the plane.

A rather bombastic gentleman called Dave booked to stay for Bed Breakfast and

Evening Meal for one year, four nights a week for a local contract he had taken. I didn't do many evening meals after Clare was born but four nights a week for one year was a good regular income which was sorely needed after we had to buy the farm when the interest rates where at their height. This was during the early 2000's because the Harry Potter films and books were at their peak. In the evenings Clare would take the food through to the dining room for me and he would talk to her. Well he knew and had seen everything; his wife was a stunning Swedish beauty, according to him. Clare came back into the kitchen one night and, as he wasn't a Harry Potter fan and she was concerned he might hear her, she said 'Dobby had to iron his fingers'. If you haven't seen the films or read the books Dobby was a house elf who had to obey his owner and, if he had bad thoughts about his master he used to 'iron his fingers' as a punishment. This became our catch phrase during that year. One weekend his 'stunning Swedish beauty' came to stay with him. What a shock, she was short, solid built and very plain, and we had worked ourselves up to see a stunner. Dobby had to iron his fingers yet again.

Another smart young gentleman stayed with us for a few weeks, four days a week and got quite chatty with us. Although he had a full-time job he also had ambitions to run his own business. At home, in his garage, he was experimenting with how to turn used Chip Shop oil into a fuel which could be used in cars. Alternative fuels where quite a new concept in the 1980's. Every Monday he would come up with an update on his experiments. He was convinced that this would be a viable proposition as the chip shops would be glad to dispose of their old oil if it cost them nothing, he just had to collect it and treat it. He had a cunning plan as to how he was going to try out the new 'fuel'. He was going to hire a car and put the 'fuel' in so that his own car wouldn't be at risk of breaking down! We were not so sure that the hire company would like this idea if they knew about it but we never did find out how the plan had gone as he moved on to pastures new.

CHAPTER 12
FRIENDS

I must also say 'and family' as when we were very busy I had to book in rooms for the children to stay when they came home. For five years Jennifer and her husband Gareth lived in Inverness and when they came home I had to make sure they had a room to stay in. Children's parties would always be organised when we had no guests staying. When Clare was in her teens sleep overs were the order of the day and I made sure they were 'booked in' when we had no other guests about as 'sleep' is not on the agenda. A number of our friends would stay with us when they visited from different parts of the country and it was always a please to see them. Big family parties were held over Christmas when I could seat 25 in the dinning room for a sit-down meal. The biggest party we had was a house warming party after the builders had finished the alterations. We invited family, friends, builders etc not forgetting the bank manager. Seventy people joined us that evening for a buffet and the house wasn't crowded. We also held parties for the Wine Club we were members of as well as other organisations.

Very few guests became close friends, but we keep in touch with some to this day, mainly on Facebook.
In August 2004 I had an email from Mrs. Hockenhull wanting to visit a friend in the area. Now this is my maiden name and so when I emailed her back saying I had a vacancy I asked if she was related to the Cheshire Hockenhull's. It turned out that her husband was the grandson of my great grandfather's brother. We where related, this generation of the family had twelve children and I am a descendent of the second son and he was a descendent of the second to youngest son. We were and still are both interested in tracing the family tree. Our family bible goes back to 1700 but she had gone back another hundred years with the tree and so we still exchange information and Christmas cards and keep in touch.

In the spring of 2003 Katie McManamus arrived on our door step. She was contracted to work for ten days a month for a local curtain making firm, Montgomery Tomlinson in Sealand, just outside Chester. They had offered to pay for her to stay in a hotel but she wanted somewhere more personal as it's not always pleasant for women to sit in hotel dining rooms on their own. Katie and I became firm friends. We would go to see 'girly' films together in an evening and swap books to read. She was an avid reader and a big Harry Potter fan. Her job was building web sites. We were such good friends that when we went on holiday she would stay to feed the dogs and look after the house for us. This was all fine until the day we forgot to leave her the key to get in. She rang us on her mobile and we had great fun trying to explain the hiding place in the dairy for our spare key. She had trouble reaching it with one hand holding her phone but she succeeded in the end. She later became 'self employed' although she still worked for Montgomery's and I started to do her accounts for her and sort out her VAT. Her mother lived in Cambridgeshire and she would be driving from her home in Selby, Yorkshire to us and then down to Cambridgeshire. As her mother became frailer into her eighties it became quite a chore and her mother suggested that she sold her bungalow and moved up to be near Katie. She bought a bungalow near Runcorn in 2009, close to Katie's work to save her travelling so much. We then became close friend of her mother as well and often visited each other. It was interesting to hear her mother's tales of the war years in London. I do remember one story she told of her and her friend dressed up and, on their way, to church one Sunday morning when they heard a German plane above them. There was nowhere to shelter, only a shop doorway which they shared with two young men. The bombs where dropped so close to them that the glass in the shop window shattered and dust was everywhere but there wasn't so much as a scratch on any of them. They did have to go home to change as they were just too dusty and not fit for a church service. After her mother died Katie sold the house in Runcorn and moved jobs nearer home. She and I would then get on the train and meet up in Manchester for some retail therapy. Katie and I do still keep in touch on Facebook and by phone, I expect we will always be friends. She is probably the only guest that I will say that about.

Roger White joined us while house hunting in the area in 1992 and eventually he, his wife and three boys bought a new house in the estate next to the farm. Over the next ten Wendy would book guest in to stay with us who were doing business with Roger or visiting them as family or friends. Wendy and I became firm friends and they let me use their computer when I was on the computer course as I didn't have one at that time. One day she had planned to go to see Swan Lake in Liverpool with her neighbour

but the neighbour had to back out through illness and so I was invited to go. I dressed smartly for the occasion, navy blue suit with a straight skirt and stiletto heels, and walked across the field, climbed the five-bar gate and walked up to the estate to Wendy's house. She just found this so funny she couldn't stop laughing to think I'd climbed a gate in my best cloths; well its what farmers do. Later Wendy, Roger and the children emigrated to near Niagara Falls in Canada but we still keep in touch.
David Evans was another customer who stayed while house hunting. His wife and children were still in Herefordshire and his new job was on the Deeside Industrial Estate.

Dave was a very quiet man and when Mandy, his wife, came house hunting I asked her if he was happy with his accommodation. She said that he was as he'd stayed somewhere else when he first moved up but complained to Mandy and she had found us. They later bought a house in Hope and we pop in to see them if we are passing. They even came to our house warming party, when we moved into the bungalow.

One of our farmer friends, Brynley Williams, became a Welsh Assembly

Member in 1999 after he had become the ring leader of the farmer's tractor blockage of Stanlow Oil Refinery when the price of oil went through the roof, and he had been interviewed on the television. Over the next few years I would meet him on various local committees, especially the committees to do with the 'right to roam' debates as to which land would be opened up for public access. At the same time Jane Hutt became an assembly member and was given the job of Minister for Health. When Ministers visited North Wales at that time they would often stay in a hotel called Kinsale Hall a couple of miles down the road in Mostyn, which has now closed. The drivers and secretaries would stay with me. It was common for me to have big black ministerial cars parked in our car park. I was talking to one of the drivers one night and he was telling me he had seeing Brynley walk out of the Assembly buildings carrying a portable TV. Now Brynley was quite a private person who would never in a month of Sundays steal and so the chauffer had teased him by asking him if that was what he was doing leaving with a television. A month later I was sat by Brynley in a meeting in County Hall, Mold, and asked him about the 'stolen' TV. His face said it all, 'How the hell did you know about that living up here?' he asked. 'I have my contacts' I replied before going on to explain how I'd heard the story. I might not have gone out to work but I certainly knew what was going on in the world as the world came to me.

After our helper, Claire, left us her sister Sharon took up the reins until she also moved on, left school and got a job. When Claire got married they spent their wedding night in our best ensuite room. We added champagne, flowers and chocolate for them. She forgot a change of cloths and so came down to breakfast in her wedding dress.

I managed on my own, with the help of the girls, for a number of years until Clare was born. As she was born in August, a busy time of year for guests, I was in need of help again and so John set off to gather money on the milk round and to find me a helper. He came back with Gwyneth. He'd asked if any of her three daughters would like to help as her oldest daughter, Nerys, already helped on the milk round. For a few years we had found that having two milk round helpers worked better, the children could take it in turns, a week off and a week on as it was an early start for them before school. Gwyneth didn't want to wait on table, she didn't do 'talking to the public' but she was a good cleaner and knew all the local gossip, that's always worth a lot. She came in one day a week to give the house total clean and other days as I needed her, to change beds. There were only two problems with Gwyneth. She did love to try out the perfumes in the guest's bedrooms. I do hope none of them noticed that some was missing. Her other 'problem' was when she dusted the dinning room. She was very much a creature of habit, once she'd started to do a job one way you couldn't change it. The dining room was oak panelled up to about four-foot-high, just over a meter in modern measurements. On the top of the panelling was a narrow ledge which I decorated with small ornaments. Gwyneth would pick up the first ornament with her left hand, dust and put the ornament down crossing her left hand over the right hand and repeat this along the full length of the seven-meter-long room on both sides and across the four meters of the back wall. The consequence of this was that the ornaments moved until it was obvious that there were more at one end than the other. I would look at the room and think there were ornaments missing. When I put the ornaments there I put one over each down panel of the panelling. In all the years she helped me I couldn't stop her doing this how many times I politely explained the plan to her. I never had one of these small ornaments stolen although a customer did once ask if she could buy one off me as she collected anything to do with libraries and this was a small animal holding a book.

I can’t finish this chapter without mentioning my best friend, Judith, who has supported me through thick and thin, especially through three miscarriages between having Jennifer and Clare. There is a thirteen-year age gap between them. Whenever we needed a break we would visit Abakan for coffee and cream scones, a good natter and a walk round the fabrics and knitting wools. We could always find something to laugh about especially on the occasion when I needed material for a little black dress for a special occasion. I chose the fabric but it was very fine and so I decided that I would make the body of the dress double thickness and the sleeves single. This would take five metres of fabric plus a black zip. The ‘floor’ girls cut the fabric and we walked to the counter with the fabric and zip. The girl on the counter asked me how much the fabric was and I told her it was 85p a metre. One of the other staff called her and she crossed the floor to answer their question and then came back. She looked at the till and said, eighty-five pence wasn’t it. Judith heard this and shot out of the door, she had just burst out laughing. I had to stand there with a straight face and pay eighty five pence for what turned out to be a smart A line black dress with roll collar and long sleeves with a small rolled cuff edge but split from top to bottom with just a catch of thread at the elbow. She came with me on my first tourism course in the agricultural college in Ruthin in 1981 and even did B&B herself for a couple of years before moving on to other things. The Ruthin course was great fun, especially as one lady, who had stables, always sat at the back and fell asleep after lunch. It was always good to get around a table with other guest house owners and compare notes. Judith was originally from Bolton and her friend, Susan and husband Alex have stayed with us more than once. Judith had moved to Colwyn Bay in the 1970's to take the job of entertainment officer in the Methodist Holiday Home. She took people out on bus trips and walks up Snowdon. She told me that one week she had had great difficulty trying to entertain that week's customers, she couldn't raise a smile from them so she decided to have a bit of fun with them herself. On the bus drive to Anglesey, as you drive through the tunnels near Conway Castle, you get a good view of both Anglesey and Puffin Island. Standing out from the water between the two there is what looks like a long metal pole. She told me that she nudged the drive and told him just to agree with everything she said. She then proceeded to point out the metal rod to the people on the bus, explaining to them that it was the conning tower of the submarine belonging to the Welsh Nationalist party but that they had run out of diesel and couldn’t afford to fill it up to move it. This greatly concerned her party who spent the rest of the week asking her if it had been moved.

CHAPTER 13
HOBBIES

We had numerous odd 'hobby' participants staying over the years including a team of bell ringers, or to go by their correct name, campanologists.

We had a deaf gentleman and his wife staying, at the time when we still shared a sitting room with guests. Susan and Jennifer where fascinated with his Braille watch and books. His hobby was listening to and identifying bird songs. He had a parabolic reflector, a big round dish, which he put on the bedroom window sill and he could hear the birds as far away as Hilbre Island. His wife was a teacher and she taught Susan and Jennifer to recite the poem; 'Tiger Tiger burning bright, in the forest of the night'. They can still recite it now.

In 2006 the Open Golf Championship was at Hoylake on the Wirral. I was fully booked for months before hand and it was weather wise, a wonderful week. In fact it was so hot that our guests decided it was better to be there for the early tee off and come away in the afternoon and so they went without breakfast. As they hadn't booked evening meals it was an easy week for me.

We gave them our directions and told them not to follow the signs as it was taking them the long way around and onto much busier roads, they were very grateful for this. It was a pleasure to have people in who were happy with what they were doing. Some of them even got pictures with and autographs from their favourite players.

Before that, in August 1995 we had the five members of the under 18's Swedish golf team and their captain, Miss Eva Flodberg staying for a competition at the Northop Country Club, just up the road. We also had some of Dave Bumbry's team staying at thc same time. One of them said he'd got a serious problem with his glasses and they kept steaming up due to the sight of some many good-looking girls in shorts. They had requested a special sort of bread and so I had to hunt it out and, luckily, I was able to buy it locally. They went on to win the competition with the French coming second. I said how pleased I was that they had beaten the French and went on to explain that as a whole the British were not too keen on the French. They said that that explained why they had so much applause, they hadn't understood why everyone was so pleased when they won as the audience was mainly British people.

Holywell Swimming Baths and Leisure centre regularly had Welsh swimming competitions for the national children's swimming leagues. This would result in mums, dads, and swimmers staying on a number of weekends though out the year, but usually in January from 1994 onwards for about ten years. This was a handy booking as it didn't clash with holidays. The parents were almost more competitive than the children. Holywell also held Badminton competitions and was part of the Welsh Badminton league with participants staying with us. We had the Welsh Badminton advisor, Mike, to stay with us about twice a year on his rounds of Welsh clubs, the local club also being based in the Holywell Leisure Centre. Squash was another sport practised in the Leisure centre and we would have the Squash Wales representative, staying once a year along with regular squash competitors.

Fishing competitions and fishermen where another group who came under the heading of 'Hobbies'. In 1992 there was a fishing competition in the Greenfield Valley just down the road and competitors stayed with me. Also in Mostyn there was a trout farm run by Von, she would sometimes send her fisher men up to stay with me. She was also a member of both Delyn and later Flintshire Tourism Associations.

Wats Dyke was the original border line between England and Wales which ran from Basingwerk Abbey in the north down for 40 miles into Shropshire and it was one of the walks for the more adventurous guests along with Offa's dyke which covered over 170 miles down to the Seven estuary. Both built in another age of wars between two peoples. I've waved guests off on their walk from Greenhill in all sorts of weather but never envied them the walk. It's not my sort of fun after a hard days work. I thought I would stick to the 'home brewing' and later playing first a Tenor Horn, then a Cornet and later a Trumpet in various bands.

We had many people staying because of their hobbies; some were quite unusual hobbies like the father and son who stayed with us twice to take pictures of buses. When a company bought a new bus they would take its picture in the company's colours and then, as the buses were sold on they would follow them and take more pictures in the new colours.

On one occasion in 2011 we had horse owners with their horses for two nights as there was a local gymkhana they wanted to compete in. The horses were old hands and very laid back and we put them in a field on there own near the house, but our cows were not so sure about them having never seen horses before. They lined up along the hedge and watched the horses for over two hours before wandering off to eat and sleep.

We did have a milk bottle collector staying who had to buy one of our bottles with our name on and look through the rest of the bottles to see if we had any with other names. People would buy milk on holiday and take the bottles home to put out for their own milk man and, believe it or not, there was a 'bottle recovery' man whose job it was to return your bottles to you and take away any other bottles you had. You had to pay a fee for yours and this was how he made his living. We finished bottling our own milk in 1993 as we could see that the supermarkets where taking our trade and the guest house trade had grown to a point where it needed more time spent on it.

I had a school inspector staying on a number of occasions when he was working in North Wales. He had to travel up from

Mid Wales and inspections can take a day or two as I know from my experience as a school governor and Chair of the Home School Association in our local High School. On one occasion I felt as though I had been truly inspected when I was grilled by an inspector on my work with the home school association. Not wanting to upset the school's reputation I failed to tell the inspector that the Home School association had had to hand over two hundred pounds plus towards the printing costs of all the 'statements' for children with learning difficulties just so that the inspectors could read them just once. Anyway, my inspector guest had an unusual hobby. He trained heavy horses to work pulling logs and then working them up to pulling the old fashion farm machinery. I expect that he needed to get out in the fresh air after all the hot air generated during inspections.

Over the years many people stayed on their quest to track down their ancestors. Mrs. Dickson was one such guest, whose great grandfather, a Mr. Jones, was from Holywell and had gone to the National School which was in Bryn Celyn. We were able to tell her that the site of the National School was now two semi detached houses, and so she walked down the road and knocked on the door of one of the houses. Veronica was able to show her the children's coat pegs, the timber had been re-used as part of the roof trusses when the school was demolished, and the houses built.

Another ancestor hunter was tracking down a relative who had worked for the Parry's Mine Company; this company mined for lead and had sites on Parry's Mountain in East Anglesey and in Holywell. It turned out that their great –great- grandfather had been a vagabond and a bigamist. I did wonder why they wanted to know about such a person, but it was part of their history. I'm sure we all have such people in our pasts somewhere.

We had some friends whose 'hobby' was to ring us up and pretend to book rooms but with a list of strange requests. One day they pretended that they where Arabs who wanted to bring their harem and to kill a sheep in the room to eat. I cottoned on to their 'hobby' and would often just play them along until they had to give up.

Bikes came in all sorts, shapes and sizes for all sorts of competitions. In September 2000 there was a mountain bike competition locally, at Nannerch which we went to watch after making the cyclists beds. Road bike races took place locally quite often and we had a few people on cycle holidays. The racing cyclists valued their bikes to such an extent we either had to offer them locked accommodation for their bikes or they would even take them to pieces and take them up to their rooms or leave them in the porch or the utility room as they were so valuable.

We've had some beautiful motor cycles staying at the farm over the years some of which had to be locked up as local youngsters where coming up the road taking too much interest in them and one day we had a 1930's omnibus on its way to the Llandudno Victorian fair.

John bought himself a Westfield kit car and, if the guests would pay for the petrol he would take them out in it. We did look into hiring it out but the insurance etc was prohibitive. One girl asked me if I screamed when he drove fast and I said No, he needs to concentrate. He did go too fast one day and hit the inside bank, spun the car and left me 2 foot away from a 30 foot drop and I didn't scream at all. We told the children that when we have had enough of life we are going to climb into the car and drive it over a cliff. There reply was ‘what a waste of a good car, get out and jump’. KIDS

To farmers their job is their hobby and so we would have many a happy evening talking farming with people from all over the world. One hot summer we were complaining that we had no grass for the cows and some Australian farmers told us that the last time they had a drought they fed cattle feed to their cows for 15 months. That put us in our place; we had no right to complain about one dry summer.

On another occasion we had some Yorkshire beef and pig farmers and some Norwegian beef and potato farmers at the same time. The conversation went on well into the night. People where so interesting but it could get tiring, you couldn’t sit up every night talking. This is why, when we altered the house, we had two sitting rooms, one for us and one for guests.

Some guests, especially Americans, did want to invade our space and I have had to stand in the dining room doorway and politely block their entry into our half of the house. We could also split the house into our side and the guest house and lock the middle doors, especially if we had to go out and guests where staying in. Better safe than sorry, although it was rare for us to feel uncomfortable in our own house. One guest did ask me if we had a safe, which we did, when we started out on this career most people paid with cash and, when we where renovating the middle of the house, we had a safe concreted into the office floor. Later on we got a credit card machine as fashions and needs change. When I told him we did he handed me a wad of money and asked me to keep it safe for him as he didn't want to leave it in his room. For my own security, in front of him, I put it into an envelope, sealed it and asked him to sign across the seal, that way he couldn't accuse me of taking any of it. I'm sure I was being too careful but, yet again, better safe that sorry.

On the farm where John's father, Tegid, was born there is an annual Sheep Dog Trial on the last Friday and Saturday in July. John's father was a keen follower and participant in this sport along with his uncle Gwyn. As well as the Sheep Dog Trials there is a horse show, produce tent and Terrier racing, and other craft stalls. One year we had a Swiss lady from Lucerne staying who said she would join us at the show as she had never been to one before. One of the craft stalls was embroidering sweat shirts with any picture you wanted. She was taking orders for later delivery. The Swiss lady badly wanted to buy some of these as presents and so we agreed that the sweat shirts would be delivered to us and we would take them over to Switzerland in September when we were booked to stay in Interlaken. This is what we did for a number of years, we would fly into Geneva and hired a car for the drive to Interlaken, we drove up to Lucerne one day to deliver the sweat shirts, through a very long tunnel, I think it was about ten miles long, to the town where we found our meeting place. She kindly took us to lunch in one of the local restaurants where they even stocked a big range of UK whiskies including one from the Isle of Mull where my sister lives. She walked us around the city walls and up a newly renovated bell tower. I asked if the bell still struck the hour and she said she didn't know but as we walked down the tower it struck up for 12p.m. it was rather loud when you where that close. She also showed us around the city and over the old wooden bridge which crosses the river and which has shops on it. It's a beautiful, quaint old city and well worth a visit.

In September 2008 the International Sheep Dog Trials were held in Abegele. This was a bit too far away for competitors to stay but all the accommodation around Abegele was full and this meant that people had to stay further afield. We were full up over the period. Events do make such a difference to accommodation providers and other businesses in an area.

One of the strangest 'hobby' requests we had was in 1999 when a couple told me that they had a hawk and did we have any wild rabbits on the farm which the hawk could hunt. Our farm had heavy clay soil which is difficult for rabbits to burrow into and so although we could give them a room for the night we couldn't oblige them with any rabbit.

CHAPTER 14
BALDRICK

You can believe what you want about the following stories; they are just our families and guest experiences in our old house.

We had four boys for one night, possibly two, on a cycling holiday along with another couple staying for the week with their two children. Now Greenhill was supposedly haunted. We called him Baldrick, we just hope he didn't watch the Blackadder programmes. After breakfast I told the boy cyclists about the ghost and watched their jaws drop. The wife of the other family saw it as well and joined me to escalate the story. We really shouldn't have done this as the boys left in a hurry that morning is sheer panic. It's not really good to frighten your customers away but we both had a good laugh over it.

Numerous people, including myself, have heard footsteps on the landing but when they went upstairs there was no one there and no one else in the house.
I have seen Bauldrick sitting in my front room, it was a strange experience, about one o'clock in the afternoon I was walking through to the utility room with some

washing when I saw someone sat in a chair looking out of the window, at first I thought it was a guest who had come back early and then realised I could see the cushion and then it was gone. This 'person' was a tall gentleman with long hair and a large white collar.

I also had a strange experience a few weeks before John's mother died. I woke in the middle of the night to see what I thought was smoke above the bed. In a panic I woke John who told me not to see silly as we had smoke detectors in all our bedrooms, a necessary precaution when running a guest house. A friend who went to the Spiritualist Church explained it to me as meaning that I was being warned about something and sure enough John's mother who was ill died soon afterwards.

The house always had a happy atmosphere and I just accepted what I'd seen. I only ever told guests as they were leaving so as not to put anyone off staying. Angelique and Rachel stayed with us when visiting family in Holywell who had heard about Bauldrick. The friend, Ros, sent me a thank you note in which she said that Angelique and Rachel had slept well and 'the ghost troubled them not at all'.

We had two ladies staying one night in our twin-bedded room which had an inglenook fireplace. Greenhill had been built in many parts. Originally it had been a timber framed house with a great hall and side rooms and it would have been single story. At this point it was probably the lower grange farm linked to Basingwerk Abbey. The Great Hall had been demolished and a Queen Ann style extension built with a curved bay window at the front, the back room had the great hall window in it. It was common to re use timbers and windows; many of the internal beams had all sorts of holes in them from a previous use. During the early 18th century an extension was built at the back. This consisted of a half cellar with two half rooms above it. There was an inglenook fireplace in the cellar where the beer had been brewed when the house was a pub, this fireplace had two more fireplaces above in the other two rooms and the fireplace directly above it was also an inglenook with a beautiful beam supporting it which we found had been closed in at some time. It was big enough for us to put a dressing table in it with a light above. In the nineteenth century another extension was added which was used as a stable and malting rooms for the brewery. This was the side of the house we lived in and the guests had the older side. All these extensions where built in different materials and at different levels not joined to each other and some with no foundations. At breakfast the next morning the conversation got around to ghosts. The two ladies said that they had seen a small girl sitting in the inglenook fireplace and so I told them about Baldrick and about the strange wall. A number of guests had told us that they had gone to the toilet in the night and thought they had bumped into a wall and there was nothing there. This happened at the point between the original house and the Queen Ann extension.

Well the two ladies rang me two years later to ask if they could bring some friends and hold a séance to see what other ghosts we had. They stayed on a night when we had to go out and so we left them to it. What they told us made an interesting story, believe it if you want to, who knows. Firstly there was a man on the middle landing were we heard the footsteps who didn't want to talk to anyone, a miserable person. Then there was a monk who traded children, a paedophile from the sixteen hundreds possibly linked to the Abbey. A teenage girl was in the top bedroom who told them that there was a grinding wheel where our utility room was backing onto the oldest rooms and it took twelve men to turn it. A man called John had died in the house as there had been a fire and he was lame and couldn't get out quickly enough. I'm not sure what I believe, I do know there are things out there and I can feel 'atmospheres' but I don't look into it, I accept it as it is.

We also had a man who came to us and said that he'd dreamt that he'd been a second in a duel at the front of the house and he'd never had a dream in his life before, we never did find out if a duel was ever held there but it wasn't beyond happening as the house had been a pub for many years.

Susan's husband had been kept awake by someone talking to him all night in the same room where Jennifer slept as a child and on some occasions, she said she didn't want to sleep there but never gave us a reason. We just thought she didn't want to go to bed so early.

One day a lady arrived up who had lived in Greenhill as a child and wanted to see what it looked like now. I asked her about the ghosts and she said that her Jack Russell dog would never sleep upstairs on the middle landing, he would howl all night. I then asked Johns mother about the ghost and she said that the people who lived there before them told her there was something on the landing and as they didn't use that side of the house and she didn't want to frighten the children, she didn't tell them, which explained why John knew nothing about the stories.

The Curate in St. James Church in Holywell had three daughters who had guinea pigs; he used to come up to buy hay and straw for them. His youngest daughter was in school with Clare. We told him about Baldrick and a few years later when, John Evans, the previous Vicar, retired he came back as Vicar of St. James's. When I saw him one day he said that he was now qualified to do an exorcism, and did we want Baldrick removed. As Baldrick was no trouble to anyone I said that I didn't want to throw him out of his home as he'd lived there longer than I had.

When the national Eisteddfod was taking place in Mold in 1991 we had the BBC Wales radio team staying, they were another group with a special diet, I had to make them plain yogurt. I always made my own yogurt and gave them fresh fruit and jam to add to it. As it was the first time they had all been together for some time they decided to have a Christmas Dinner in July and so they booked the occasion in the Victoria Hotel in Holywell and the owner fetched all the decorations out and made it a real Christmas treat for them with Father Christmas thrown in. One night they decided to have a bit of fun with me, I hadn't told them about Baldrick but they decided that an old house like ours must have a ghost, so they dressed up one of the reporters in a grey cloak and filmed him 'floating' around the front room and then called me in and showed me the film saying that they had left the camera running while the room was empty. I found it quite amusing especially when I went on to explain to them about Baldrick, which throw them, I had managed to turn the tables on them.

I only told guests about Baldrick as they were leaving and if I had the time to talk to them. One morning I was telling the story to middle aged couple when she visibly shook from head to toe. They then went on to talk in detail about spirits, some of which I really didn't want to hear, they were quite an odd couple and I was pleased when they left. I then went up to room number three where they had spent the night and there was a really strange atmosphere in the room, it made me want to run. I stood my ground and told the 'presence' that it was my house and I wasn't leaving for anyone and if they weren't happy they could leave. In the Chester Chronicle, the local weekly paper, the following week there was as story about the strange sighting of a lady in the pub further up the road and I did wonder if my spirit had taken my offer up and left to haunt someone else. I felt, on reflection, that the couple who had stayed that night may have been black witches.

On a different note I do have another 'ghost' story. Father Francis was quite a famous singing monk who sang at concerts though out the country. In 1985 he was living at the Monastery at Pantasaph near Holywell and was due to give a concert in the Monastery. He had invited his sisters up to hear him play and booked them in to stay with me. They duly arrived and I showed them up to their room with the father. As I came down the stairs some American guests had just returned from their day out and were sitting in the front room to write postcards. We had found oak beams behind the plaster which formed the wall between the front room and the hall and so we had opened the whole area up to make it open plan and to show off the beams. I went to talk to them and ask them how their day had gone. As we were talking Father Francis quietly walked down the stairs, across the hall and out through the front door. The poor Americans just watched this with their mouths wide open, ‘Did you see that?’ they asked, ‘Was it a ghost?’ On this occasion I was able to put their minds at rest and explain that it was a real monk.

CHAPTER 15
SERENDIPITY.

This chapter is full of different guest stories which won't fit into any other chapters easily.

Just before the Falkland's War we were still sharing our sitting room with guests and after a couple from Portsmouth had stayed we saw them on the television waving off the troop ships on the docks. Our guests were famous!

On the night the Iraq War started we had a lorry loaded with oxygen bottles in our back yard as it was too big to park in the front of the house with the other guests vehicles. This particular guest delivered gas bottles to hospitals. Poor Clare had heard the news about the first attacks by the British and American forces and was totally convinced that the gas bottles would be hit by bombs coming back from Iraq, especially as we had all heard about the 'weapons of mass destruction' on the news. Her and our bedrooms overlooked the back yard. We tried to put her mind at rest but she didn't sleep very well that night and was pleased when the lorry left.

On more than one occasion we had members of the BBC orchestra staying when they were performing in St. Asaph Cathedral. These people work at night going to bed late and getting up late. In April 1996 they stayed and we had been out for the evening. We arrived back at about the same time as the orchestra players. John told them that he was going outside to check on a cow which was close to calving and they all decided that this was a experience they couldn't miss so they all followed him outside. Half an hour later they all came back in to say that they had seen the calf being born and had seen all the other baby calves we had. They had let the calves suck their fingers and the sleeves of their suits. On stage an orchestra looks very smart in black evening dress and I was shocked to see the mess on the sleeves of the jackets. When I commented on the mess they pointed out that in fact these where there working cloths, made in machine washable polyester. What a surprise that was, they just threw them into the washing machine on a low wash after a concert. This made me think about the way different people dress. Many people go to work in a suit these days, but farmers go in work in overalls. When 'suit' people go out in an evening they dress down to relax. When farmers go out in an evening they dress up to relax, they don't want to go out in jeans as they've worn them all day. I have been sneered at for dressing 'up' by men in a pub once, the way we dress shouldn't be a cause for sneering, its personal taste.

Letting pets stay in the bedroom with their owner is personal taste on behalf of the B&B or Hotel owner. It is their prerogative as to whether to allow this or not. I've let hamsters, in their cages, stay in the utility room when guests have no one to look after them but I draw the line at animals in the bedrooms. I would never let my dogs into a room which had carpet on it never mind let them upstairs. I had a lady with a Great Dane at the door one night begging me to let her and her dog stay in the room. I always said that the dogs can stay in their owner's cars overnight but many won't do that. People staying for local sheepdog trials don't have a problem with that, their cars are set up with cages so that the dogs have everything they need. I found that if I told them that our dogs would bark all night if they thought there was another dog in the house they would accept this.

On one occasion I did let someone take their cat up to the room; they had stayed with me before and promised to keep the cat in the cage. They didn't, and the mess was appalling, it was a long-haired cat and the hair was everywhere. I all but had to spring clean the room before it was fit for anyone else to use. I've heard other B&B owners say they have had to redecorate after dogs had been let into rooms wet and dirty. That may be how people live at home but us accommodation owners have to maintain a high standard to keep our tourist board ratings, people should leave things as they find them, clean and tidy.

Clare, as a teenager, went away to London with three other girls once and made them all clean up their rooms when she saw the mess because she knew what it was like to have to clean messy rooms. We in the industry judge people by the way they leave the rooms.

A lovely sounding gentleman rang up one day to book a double room for him and his wife for one night. He didn't tell me why he was staying away but that wasn't important. I took all his details and he and his wife duly arrived on the night in question. I think I only had one other couple staying that night. Now the wife was a different kettle of fish all together. I don't think she wanted to stay at all, if it wasn't that she was deliberately causing her husband trouble. I showed them up to the room and she promptly walked straight over to the bed and pressed it up and down announcing that the mattress was too soft and didn't I have a harder one. This performance went on in every bedroom I showed her and eventually she told her husband she wouldn't be able to sleep in any of the rooms and walked down the stairs and straight out of the front door. There was nothing wrong with any of the mattresses she just didn't want to stay. The poor man was mortified as he tried to apologise to me. When things like this happen you just can' take it personally.

When Clare was in school I applied for the job of School Governor representing the pupils in our local primary school. I was duly elected to the job which, at that time, in a junior school, was not too odious. I do remember volunteering for people to buy raffle tickets at 10p a go to 'Gunk a Governor'. They put their names on the tickets and at the end of the day a ticket was drawn out. Luckily for me, it was drawn out with Clare's name on it and so she had the honour of gunking her own mother. This was the second year running this contest had been run and we had learnt by our mistakes. The bowl of 'gunk' contained plenty of shampoo and so I changed into cloths suitable for 'gunking' and after it was all over with I could wash it out of my hair with very little trouble. This was the most memorable part of my job in the junior school and so I went on to stand as Governor in the High School for which I was also elected. In all I served as a school Governor for nine years. The High School job was much more demanding. On one occasion parents had complained that one of the bus drivers was letting the children stand on the bus right up against the front windows which was dangerous. This was at a time before buses had seat belts. It was a difficult problem to solve at the time. In the end we had to move the buses so that they parked on the school land and so had to be covered by the school insurance which gave us the control to talk to the driver and stop this activity. During the time that we were trying to solve this problem I had a couple staying from Birmingham and the company the gentleman worked for had just started to import the American school buses which we see everywhere now. I tapped his brain about the subject and was able to go back to the next Governors meeting with my new found knowledge. At all senior school Governor's meetings there is a representative from the Council Education Department, there to make sure we are doing our job correctly. At the next meeting the Chair reported to us all that we had been complemented by the Education Department for the work we had done and on the amount of trouble we had gone to to find out so much information. I did learn so much from my various guests without having to leave the house.

As I've said previously, children are not really a problem; parents who don't discipline their children were my biggest problem. We did our best to keep children amused and out of mischief. We had a play area with swings and seating for parents outside. We also had a cupboard in the sitting room with games and books in for guests to use. The room which was previously a kitchen, at the far end of the house I now used as a utility room. It had the oil heating boiler a sink, my washing machine, spin drier and an old fashion drying rack which I could hoist up and down. This was particularly useful if it rained as it could hold four sheets and eight pillowcases, two beds worth of bedding. It was quite a big room and so we put in it a ¼ size snooker table and a darts board, set up on the wall on an old drop leaf table top which we painted matt black and which stopped most of the darts which missed the dart board from hitting the wall. On one occasion parents with two boys left them to play in the utility room and they gave up playing snooker and used the snooker cues to hack the plaster off the back wall leaving a large hole through to the brick work. These parents only ‘had a quite word’ with their sons when I told them what the children had done, I’d have been ashamed if my children had behaved like this. The husband said he would buy us a bag of plaster and repair the job. I accepted the bag of plaster but left it to an expert to re-skim the wall. They really didn’t see it as a major problem that their children were so out of control to even think of doing this or that they had been in the wrong for leaving their children so long with no supervision.

I did have one ‘child’ that I was really grateful to. Mum, Dad and their teenage son arrived and asked where the nearest magazine shop was as their son needed a computer magazine. I politely asked if he knew anything about computers and apparently he was a computer whizz kid. Thank the lord, my computer had gone and got itself a virus and I didn’t know what to do so I asked if their son could look at it for me and he did. I took him all evening to sort it out and mum and day where none too pleased until after breakfast the next morning when I told them they needn't pay because their son had saved my life.

We had an Indian Doctor of Science staying with his wife on their way to Holyhead to catch the ferry to Ireland. I showed them up to their room and apologised for having to leave them in a rush but that I would be up the yard in the top shed as John needed a hand to calve a cow. The husband was really interested and had to come and watch this. We had to explain every move to him through the operation. I say operation, this wasn't a caesarean birth but it was a difficult birth and we had to use a machine called a ratchet to help the calf out of the birth canal. You tie ropes to the calf's front legs, which come out first, put the frame around the cow's hips and use the ratchet a notch at a time in time to the cow's contractions. Done carefully this is a very successful way of calving cows which are carrying big calves without damaging them. I must point out that very few cows need assistance with the birth of their calves but you have to keep a close eye on them just in case.

He wasn't the only doctor we had staying. In the local hospital a facility had been built to provide cancer treatment so that patients didn't have to travel up to Liverpool and an application made for a specialist to fill the vacancy for the new department. We had a London doctor and his wife staying to look at the area. Their plan was to live in Chester and for him to drive to Glan Clwyn hospital near St. Asaph every day. They had hoped that they would only need one car. The plan was that the doctor's wife could just walk to the shops as she had done in London. They had quite a shock when they realised that none of this would be possible up here in the countryside and that two cars would be a necessity. They were really quite upset by this. I never found out if he took up the job or not.

I couple with a small baby came to stay for a few days and it cropped up in conversation that the husband had gone to the Lancaster Royal Grammar school. He was taken aback when I told him that my father had been a boarder in the same school. He was a bit of a snob and treated me as if I was below him so this fact didn't please him at all. He was also a male chauvinist pig. On the day they were leaving he sat in the garden reading his paper while his poor wife traipsed up and down the stairs with a baby in one arm and bags in the other. John was so disgusted with the man I had to forcibly stop him from having ‘words’. Yet again we needed to remember the rules.

A big company name you may recognise is Kimberly Clark who makes paper products. They moved their production facilities up to Flint from Kent. Any staff who wanted to move with the company had their accommodation paid for by the company for a month. We had quite a number of these people, a number moved into the new housing estate called Tan-y-Felin which was literally next door to the farm. Their children were in school with Clare and we also delivered milk to them. One of these men bought a house in Whitchurch, Shropshire which is about an hours drive away. In Kent he had been travelling nearly two hours to work every morning. Some of the local workers couldn’t believe him; they were not prepared to travel more than thirty minutes to a job.

A single lady from Russia, living near Moscow, stayed one night on her trip around the world working as she travelled. I wanted to know all about Russia as I’ve read a number of books on Catharine the Great and the Tsars of Russia. She told me that she had travelled from West to East on the train right across the country. This is an experience which interested me, I thought it would be a great way to see the various cultures as you cross from Europe into Asia, but she really put me off as she said as you go further east in the forest areas the clouds of gnats are so bad that you can't open the train windows and they are so thick that you can't even see the scenery. Now gnats love my blood so I now think this is a trip I will not be making.

Mr Tunnecliffe booked in to visit his older brother during September 1991. His brother was in a nursing home in Prestatyn. Mr. Tunnecliffe was well into his eighties himself. He said that when he was researching where to stay he had found us and wanted to stay with us as he and his family had lived at Greenhill in times gone by. He didn't remember it himself as he was a baby. He was kind enough to send us a picture of his family outside their next house in Prestatyn. His father had been the manager of an iron works down at Mostyn and John could remember it when it he was a child. When they opened the furnaces you could see the red glow from the farm. It was always interesting to talk to someone with such memories. John's family had lived in Greenhill longer than anyone else since the census records began, sixty five years in all. This was because it was a rented property when John's parents had moved there and for many years before and so people tended not to stay long. John's parents had rented the property and land since 1945 and bought it after it was condemned in the 1960's as it had no running water inside. John could just remember pumping water from the well in the yard and even, one very bad winter when everything was frozen, having to go down the road to carry water back for the house and the cattle.

April Fools day was a day on which we always loved to have some harmless fun. Milk customers would drive up to the yard before John had returned from the milk round and tell me that he'd taken their empty bottles but forgotten to leave any full ones, I had to send them home to look for the full one's because he would hid them. I also had the odd bit of fun with guests. We had some workmen in one year, before the smoking ban. We are not smokers and I was never keen one people smoking in the house but business is business and when I was a child my father smoked in the house. These workmen all smoked and so I walked into the dining room at breakfast time and asked them if they had seen the news, no came the reply back. I, with a straight face, seriously informed them that the tobacco plant harvest had failed and that the country was running out of cigarettes. I really don't know when I've seen such panic on someone's face, they where so relieved when I announced 'April Fools'. They took it all in good part.

Another April Fool story was when guests told me they had to leave by 9.30am for an appointment on 1st April. When they came down to breakfast I told them it was 9am when it was really 8am. That panicked them until I told them it was April Fools Day. After they left I went up to clean their room and couldn't find the key. Keys did occasionally go walk about, bedroom number three had a really bad habit of going on holiday but my address was on the key fob and they usually came home eventually. I looked high and low for this key, I always had a spare key but if I had to give that to a guest I couldn't get in to clean the room. Four days later I found the key, they had left it hooked up behind the bedroom door, when you opened the door to number four it went up against the wall and you didn't see behind it if you turned around. They had got their own back, I did laugh.

Another key moment arose when a regular guest told me he wouldn't be back until gone eleven o'clock on the Sunday night for room number one. I told him to take the key as we would manage. We had a one night booking of mum, dad, daughter and son, for room number one which was a twin room, and room number three, a double room with bathrooms across the landing. The bell rang at about one o'clock in the morning which woke us up with a start. We went down to see what was the matter and the mother, who had slept in room number one with the son, said that she'd gone to the bathroom in the night and that her son had followed her and closed the bedroom door behind him and the key was inside. We tried every key in the house, but none would open the door and so in the end we had to break the window and climb in. Later, after they had left I did think about it and was concerned that the father had been sleeping in the double bed with his fourteen-year-old daughter.

Poor bedroom number one it didn't seem to be a lucky room. I had a guest staying one evening and while he was in the dinning room eating his dinner the smoke detectors started to blare out. I dashed through and found that this gentleman had left his bedroom door open and had put his wet bath towel directly on top of the electric heater and switched it full on. Of course, it had caught fire and was burning merrily by the time I saw it and switched off the electricity at the plug, John had followed me and without speaking to each other we had dashed down stairs, he went to our kitchen and I went to the utility room. We both grabbed towels and soaked them in water to douse the flames. When we got back up to the room the gentleman in question was stood with another towel wafting the flame higher and saying 'it will go out in a minute. This gentleman then told me exactly how to claim off the insurance as he told me. 'I have experience of these things'. I bet he did if he didn't know that you increase the flames by adding oxygen to a fire. The room was so smoke damaged it took seven coats of emulsion paint to bring the paintwork back to its original colour. At this point in time all the rooms had electric heaters, it was only later, in the early 1990's what we put in an oil boiler and full central heating. When I thought about it I was disappointed that the towel hadn't dropped and burnt the carpet, we could have done with a new carpet in the room as it had been down for a number of years. Our swift actions meant that we didn't have to make an insurance claim.

Another ‘early’ experience was boiling contact lenses. This is something we don’t do in these days of disposable contact lenses and sterilizing liquids but back in the late 1970’s and early 1980’s guest would ask me if I could put the contact lenses, in their box, into a pan of boiling water and boil them for a minimum of twenty minutes. It wasn’t unusual for me to have a pan of contact lenses boiling next to a pan of boiling eggs on the cooker in a morning.

Easter arrives, and it is the time when I get my first ‘busy period’ of the year. When families were booked in I would decorate Cadburys Creme Eggs for the children on Easter morning. These always went down a treat and help to make stays memorable for families. I also had small knitted hats for boiled eggs if they were requested.

Most people just wanted the treat of a full cooked breakfast and so at first I only had a small, four cup, poached egg pan. One morning I did have a party of six youngsters who ordered two poached eggs on toast each, twelve eggs in total. That was a bit of a marathon which caused Claire much amusement as she stood watching me rush eggs in and out of my small poacher. After this experience I went out and bought a catering size poaching pan. The only problem was that the egg holders were metal and not 'non-stick' and were a nightmare to clean. This was another occasion when Claire, my helper, couldn't work for laughing.

I had a 'phone-call' from my local Tourist Information Centre one morning to see if I had vacancies for two single rooms for two business men. I took the booking and waited for their arrival from Manchester Airport in a taxi. It turned out that one had flown in from USA and the other from Germany to hold a business meeting and wanted to hold the meeting somewhere quiet in the countryside. The weather was good and so they spent two very special days with their paperwork spread out on the garden table while I fed them breakfast lunch and dinner. They then set off back to the airport to fly home. Now that's the way to do business.

Mrs Thackeray arrived up in the summer of 1989 with her directions taped to her steering wheel and her son, James in his child seat in the back of the car. She was a single mother having lost her husband in a car accident before James was born. He was a similar age to Clare and they had great fun playing together which gave both me and

Mrs. Thackeray a break. She was a teacher in a Yorkshire mining village and she told me that one day she realised that the children didn't have anything to cover their cloths when they where painting and so she took into school some of her husband's shirts. These shirts started to disappear and then re-appear on the children as if they were their own cloths. The children were stealing them and their mums where using them as their children's clothes. This was some years after the big mine closures and redundancies but there were still some very poor families about.

Politics is one subject you seriously try to avoid with guests as people can get very heated over their views but on one occasion I did get involved but I didn't start the subject. During the 1980's, when Margret Thatcher was Prime Minister and the recession was digging in a gentleman who was travelling on his own, cornered me in the hall and started forth for almost half an hour ranting about the lack of jobs for youngsters caused by Margret Thatcher and her Government. Now I'm an independent soul, I've made myself a job out of nothing but a big, derelict house which planners had advised us to knock down due to its poor condition. Our children had learned to work from an early age, delivering milk, and most importantly, learning how to talk to people and how to be polite and mix with all age groups. Eventually, with plenty of jobs pressing and time moving on, I turned to this gentleman and calmly said; 'It was my choice to have children, it is my job to make sure they are brought up fit and able to work not the Governments'. This is something I strongly believe; all our children know what hard work is and I get so frustrated even now when people don't pull their weight when they are working.

Lots of parents want to stay on a farm so that their children can see where food comes from and watch the cows being milked. Lots of children just want to play on someone else's swing and in the utility room on the snooker table. Many a happy evening was spent by families were the parents could relax watching TV knowing that the children where safely in the next room playing snooker or darts. Some of the parents had very little knowledge of how their food was produce which lead to one lady telling me that it was a good job we had the cows otherwise the grass would get long. I do wonder sometimes how people's minds work or even if they do work!

CHAPTER 16
WEDDINGS.

We had many weekend guests staying to go to weddings. Often we would have a house full of people who knew each other and were all ready for a party. If the bookings had been made by the local family you would usually visit to 'vet' me and see if I was 'suitable'. These guests were easy as they didn't need me to entertain them. The only problem was getting them out of bed on Sunday morning for breakfast. Breakfast would often run late which was understandable but difficult as we considered Sunday afternoons as 'our time' the only time we would get off in the week. Sunday night is a quiet night for all accommodation providers. The workers won't be back until Monday and the holiday people have to be home to get ready for work on Monday and so bed making wasn't quite such a rush job. John and I both worked seven day a week jobs and it was not unusual for us to go weeks without even an afternoon off. We accepted it as par for the course.

On one occasion a party arrived up for a wedding and it included the child bridesmaid. A dress had been given to her when she arrived but it didn't fit and mum didn't know what to do, she was in a real flap. I sat up until eleven o'clock at night altering the dress for them, for which they were very grateful. It was all in a day's work, keeping the customer happy.

On another occasion we had the bridegroom's family and the best man staying for an April wedding. They all got up early on the Saturday morning and sat in the dinning room eating breakfast when it started to snow. They all commented on how pretty it looked and we said not to worry as, being so close to the sea, snow didn't stay for long, the sea air with the salt in it would soon sort it out. It did most of the time but if the snow was heavy and the weather cold we could have a few problems. This turned out to be one of those occasions. The snow didn't stop, the wedding was to take place at Halkyn church which was higher up than we where at only a hundred feet above sea level, Halkyn must be at about eight hundred feet above sea level. The snow there was deeper than it was at Greenhill. The guests left for the eleven o'clock wedding with no trouble at out end but at Halkyn it was a different story. The bride lived higher up than the church where the snow was even deeper. The wedding car couldn't even get to her house and, of all things; she had to travelled to the church in a JCB digger! After the service and the reception it was still snowing and so the family decided to come back to us at about four in the afternoon for a rest before the evening party. At Greenhill the snow was quite deep and, when you came up the road there was quite a sharp left-hand bend before the road started to rise uphill again. This was always a problem if it snowed and poor John had to take the tractor down and tow their cars up the final incline to the house. Only the best man ventured out again for the evening party, he did manage to get back during the evening, on foot leaving his car down the road.

Our local vet, Sharn, was getting married to a local farmer. She was originally from just over the border in Scotland and so all her family were coming down to stay with us. We had her mother and father and other close relatives staying with us and they were greatly excited. They had never seen Sharn in a dress before and they had high hopes of actually seeing her legs. It wasn't to happen. Yes they saw her in a dress but no she didn't reveal her legs however a good time was had by all and she went on to have three daughters and we still keep in touch with her and Edward although they now live back over the border. In fact she has stayed with us when visiting family and friends back here in North Wales.

My friend Jude got married in 2008 and booked in some of her guests. She had also had friends staying with us for her big 0 birthday party in 2004. For her wedding I gave her a wedding cake for a present and we planned it all together, deciding how she wanted the cake iced and decorated. For this cake I think I made an icing imitation of her bouquet along with decorations around the sides. At the wedding, after the cutting of the cake ceremony the hotel took the cake into the kitchens to cut. One of the staff came to Jude and asked her who had made the cake and I was introduced. The hotel said it was one of the best cakes they had ever cut. They always took the cake back to the kitchen because often when it was cut it wasn't very nice inside. I was so pleased to help to make their day special. I told the staff who I was and the result of this was that even the local hotel sent me customers when they were full. My reputation was such that I often had recommendations from far superior accommodation than mine.

There are a number of overseas doctors working locally, especially in our local big hospital at Bodelwyddan, near St. Asaph. An

Indian couple who worked at Bodelwyddan hospital where getting married and we had some of the guests staying with us for the weekend. It was a wonderful sight on the morning of the wedding as all the female guest wore saris. I especially loved the green sari with golden threads running through it. The gold that they all wore was simply magnificent. I've never seen anything so bright and rich looking before until I went to my nephew's wedding as he also married an Indian girl a number of years later. She wore a beautiful red sari and the bridegroom, and his supporters wore cream Indian suits at a Hindu ceremony followed a few days later by a Church wedding when the bride wore a traditional white wedding dress. They had best of both worlds.

All of us 'local' B&Bs worked together to make sure everyone who needed a bed in the area got one. My nearest B&B neighbour up in Carmel was going on holiday and so she gave my name to some wedding guests. I had eight members of a family booked in to stay with me for this wedding. The week before the wedding I was walking along my back path with a bunch of rhubarb in one hand and a calving knife in the other hand when I fell over on my left ankle. A stone on the path had thrown my footing. I've gone over on my ankles many a time when delivering milk and rushing around a corner and thought it was just a strain. I sat for a while in the hope that it would settle, poor Clare made the tea and turned the rhubarb into a crumble for me. I ate my tea and, to try and ease the pain, purely for medicinal purposes, I had a couple of glasses of wine. That didn't work and in the end Clare insisted on taking me to A&E where I had my ankle X-rayed and they found a small fracture in one of the ankle bones. I then saw a doctor who told me I had to have it plastered. I told him I'd tried getting plastered but it didn't work. He didn't even smile. I then explained that I was going on holiday in six weeks time and so he said that, as it was such a small fracture he would take the plaster off after five weeks if I was careful. Well I would promise anything wouldn't I, just so I could go on holiday. I went home and told John that the bad news was I'd broken my ankle but the good news was that I'd only got one break. When I was two and a half years old I had been run over by a tractor with metal cogs not rubber tyres. On that occasion I had had three breaks and a gash in my right leg and three months in hospital on traction. I've had white coat phobia ever since. The problem then was what to do with eight guests? Everyone else I rang was too full to add eight more guests to their bookings and so I had to carry on regardless. I tried going around the kitchen on our office chair but I fell off it twice and was banned from using it by the rest of the family. I hobbled on. I went up and down stairs on my bottom and Clare and John did what they could in between their jobs. One of the wedding guests asked me how I managed to sleep with the plaster on. I said I was sleeping better than ever; I was so tired trying to drag my plastered leg around.

The daughter of one of our milk customers was getting married in June 1989 and so they came to see our accommodation before booking it for the bridegroom's family. These particular milk customers where rather fussy, their house and garden where perfect and they wanted to make sure that our accommodation was up to their standard. It must have been as they booked in thirteen of the groom's family. The bridegroom was the youngest of a large family and we had his mother, father, brothers, sisters and partners. I could only really take twelve guest but mum and dad said that their youngest daughter, who was only eight, could share their bed so that the family could stay together. On the Saturday morning many of them came down to breakfast very casually dressed. Not a surprise thinks me as I expected them to change before the service is St. James's church on the hill. NO the men went to the service dressed in Bermuda shorts in various very bright colours. The bedrooms where appalling, there was even drinking chocolate running down the outside of the sink in the bathroom. It took all morning to clean them, I was dreading Sunday as my cousin and her husband where coming for lunch and to look at our car which they wanted to buy, and I had guests booked for the Sunday night which was unusual. I set all the tables for breakfast on Saturday night with a heavy heart. It was worse than I could have imagined. At eight in the morning the groom's father came down and knocked on the kitchen door. He announced that another guest's car had broken down and he had let them sleep on the floor in the bedrooms without even asking me, there would be nineteen for breakfast. Yes, that was six more people than I was booked to cater for. What a nightmare, luckily Susan and Jennifer where there to help but by the time we had finished we had no cooked breakfast ingredient for ourselves as I only had half a rasher of bacon left, no eggs or sausages. They offered to pay, and I certainly made them pay for everything. When they left the place was even worse than on the Saturday morning. It took the three of us an age to sort things out and so we concentrated on the rooms we needed for that night. There was no way we could do all the washing and dry it, which consisted of two sheets, four pillow cases and four towels for every bed. They had used everything. I left the girls to it while I sorted out lunch for my cousin but by the end of the day we were all absolutely shattered. On the Monday evening the bride's mother came to visit us to apologize. She told us that some other members of the groom's family had stayed in the new home the couple had bought and decorated ready to move in. They had left a tub of margarine on the kitchen windowsill, on its side and the sun had melted it and it had run down and ruined the new kitchen cupboards. She was in tears, not only had they not dressed for a wedding they hadn't even bothered to buy wedding presents. The poor lady was distraught by it all after she'd put so much work in to make a beautiful day for her daughter and son-in-law.

One milk customer booked some family into our guest house for their daughter's wedding while explaining to us that they had had to work out which relatives spoke to which and put them in difference guest houses to keep the peace. They must have got it right as no fights broke out in our house.

In 1981 Prince Charles married Lady Diana Spencer and for this special occasion we had bought our first colour television for our sitting room. I bought souvenir soaps for the guest's bedrooms and souvenir serviettes for the dining room. On the big day we invited the guests to come to our small sitting room to watch the wedding on the colour TV. Us ladies got ourselves comfortable and switched on the TV while the men went out for the day, not interested in the spectacle. John was working outside. He was washing the milk bottles for the milk round. This was done in a big lumbering noisy electric machine with a hot and cold tub of water. You had to put a metal frame over the milk crate, turn the crate and frame over and slide it first into the hot and then into the cold water and jets would wash out and rinse the bottles. This took a great deal of electric power and so as soon as he switched on the machine the colour TV cut out. We only had single phase electricity to the farm when we really needed three phase for such a big machine. I had to dash off and route out the old portable black and white TV which we put on top of the colour TV and had to make do with that picture until the bottle washing job was finished so that we could all enjoy the proceedings in brilliant colour.

We sometimes had people staying who were on their honeymoon and one such couple stayed with use towards the end of our careers. She was a German doctor specialising in geriatric patients and he was a Swiss scientist working on the Hadron Particle Collider based in Switzerland. He was particularly disappointed because, while he was away the Collider had had more 'collisions' that it had ever had and he had missed them.

CHAPTER 17
DEATH AND ILLNESS.

Let me start by saying I've never had a guest die in the house but I have had people taken ill. That's not to say that people may have died in the house in the past. I do know of one lady who had her appendix taken out in one of the bedrooms when she lived in Greenhill as a child. It was common to have these operations done at home as I remember my father telling me his sister had her tonsils taken out on the kitchen table and he was upset because he wasn't allowed to watch!

An Australian couple were on a UK cycling holiday when the wife took ill in the night with appendicitis. She was a nurse and knew full well what was the symptoms were. Her husband got up and rang the bell but we were sleeping so well we didn't hear it. In desperation they went across to the bungalow on the lawn and knocked on the door where John's parents lived. His parents rang us up and we heard the telephone and got up. They didn't know what telephone number to phone in an emergency in the UK and so we called an ambulance and off they went. Now if you know anything about doctors you know that you don't tell them what you have got, that's their job and so when they got to the Accident and Emergency department and explained what the problem was the doctor told her she had an ovarian cyst and sent her in an ambulance to the maternity hospital which was about ten miles from the main hospital. The next day they got another ambulance and took her back to the main hospital where they took out her appendix. It was a good job we had a pickup as we had to ferry their bicycles around from one hospital to another and find the husband a B&B nearer the hospital. I don't think they finished their holiday on the bicycles.

One summer's morning I received a phone call from a gentleman who, with his wife, was booked in for that night. He sadly had to inform me that he had woken up in the B&B they had stayed at overnight to find his wife dead by his side. He told me he was ringing me as he was waiting for the police etc. to arrive .up, as it was an unexpected death the police where involved and, at some point, an inquest would have to take place. I sympathised with him and told him that I fully understood why he had to cancel. As a gesture of good will I returned his deposit. My next 'death' cancelation was very different. A fortnight before a booking for four adults was due to arrive for a one night stay I got a phone call to tell me that there would only be two staying and they would explain later. When they arrived they told me their sorry story. When they had decided to come to the UK from Australia on holiday some acquaintances asked if they could come along as they had always wanted to visit the UK but felt themselves too old to travel on their own. The arrangements were made and they flew into London airport and spent their first few days visiting the sights of London. The plan was then to set off around the UK first by train and then by hire car. They went to St. Pancras station to catch the train and the elderly wife dropped dead on the station. I have to admit that, at this point in the story I just wanted to burst out laughing, my first thought was, it was good job she wasn't on the train when she died because she wouldn't have a 'place of death' for the death certificate if that had happened. Because the two couples where not related the insurance company wouldn't pay for the younger couple to cancel their trip and so they had to stay in London and organise for the body and her husband to be flown back to Australia. They then had to sit down and work out where they could catch up with the original trip and cancel the rest. They were obviously traumatised by the whole event and I don't really know why I found it so funny but I did manage to keep a straight face during their stay.

Occasionally guest would book it to go to a funeral and in July 2009 a party of Irish people had travelled over the water and booked to stay with me for a local funeral. Apparently there was a party around the open coffin in the house before the service and another party after the service which carried on until after midnight. This was a traditional Irish Wake. Full cooked farmhouse breakfasts were not the order of the day the next morning!

A friend of mine who had a guest house near Bet-s-y-Coed had guest staying for a funeral and after the service they returned to change before going out for dinner. My friend heard a terrible noise upstairs and raced up to find a fight between a brother and sister going on on the landing. Yes they were fighting over the will.

A less funny 'death' story was when two young men arrived in 2007 at about eleven in the morning and knocked on the back door looking for a room. Our back door was a stable door and so I just opened the top of it to answer the knock. A young man in a peaked cap was standing there and another man was in the car which had already turned around and was facing down the road, sideways across the back drive. I said I was sorry but that I was full that night, which was the truth. Sometimes, if I didn't like the looks of someone I would say that, it didn't sound as bad as 'no I don't like the looks of you'. He asked if there was any other accommodation locally and I told them about another lady in Holywell but he said they had been there and she was full. He wasn't very happy and said goodbye and they left. John came down the yard and asked what they wanted as the boy looked familiar. He came in for coffee and to read the daily paper properly as he'd only glanced through it earlier, we read the Liverpool Daily Post. On the front page was a picture of the boy from the back door, him and his friend where wanted in connection with a murder in Huyton, Liverpool and had been spotted in Colwyn Bay in a Silver car, John had to go out for something and so I rang the local police station and told them what had happened. Thirty minutes later two plain cloths police men arrived at the back door and asked me all about the men and then went to see the other B&B lady. Another thirty minutes passed and two more plain cloths policemen arrived. They explained that they were a higher rank than the other two men. They wanted to know about the car the men where driving, now I'm not good with cars, they all have five wheels as far as I'm concerned and so I had to ring John as I knew where he was visiting and ask him to come home. He soon arrived back and gave the men all sorts of details about the car although it was parked sideways on he knew what the make and colours where although we couldn't see the number plate. We never did find out if they caught the men but I was so relieved that I was full that night.

Another group of guests arrived up one member short with the story that one of the gentlemen had fallen in Carlisle and broken his leg. They just left him in hospital and carried on with their holiday. They were members of the Rotary Club in America and had contacted the club in Carlisle and left him in the kind hands of club members who had promised to visit him to keep him company for the duration of his stay in hospital.

A couple and their two adult sons arrived one year to see family and trace long lost relatives. The husband took me to one side to tell me that, during the war his wife had moved away from North Wales and they had met and married and now lived near his family in East Anglia. She had never been back to North Wales since marrying but now she had cancer and it was her last wish to go back to Wales and see some of the places she remembered from her childhood days. The men all took such trouble to make sure she was well and that she got to see everything she wanted. Just over a year later the men returned with her ashes to scatter at a place of her choice. Such a happy yet sad story, I was so pleased to be part of making her last wishes come true.

When Clare was about eighteen or nineteen and was about to start her nurse training we had a couple staying who lived on the Isle of Wight. Their son lived in Holywell and they had booked in to visit him and his wife and children. We got chatting and she told us that she had nearly died of Streptococcal Fasciitis. This is otherwise known as the flesh-eating disease and is an infection which results in the death of the body's soft tissue. It is a severe disease which starts very suddenly and spreads rapidly, usually starting on the limbs. It gets into the skin through small cuts or even burns and shows up as red or purple patches and fever. In her case it had attacked her upper arm and she was quite happy for Clare to inspect the loss of muscle it had caused which made her arm look malformed. This couple stayed with us a number of times whilst visiting their son and she would show her disfigured arm and tell her story to anyone who was interested. Clare and Jennifer both took a great interest being both members of the nursing profession. Susan and I where a little more squeamish and didn't want to look.

Occasionally I would have to make a doctors appointment for a guest, usually for something minor or if they had run out of their regular prescription. They were always amazed that after their visit they would offer to pay or hand over their insurance details but
these were always refused by the local surgery, they where always treated for free.

In October 1997 guests booked in for one night on their way west for a week in a cottage. There were granny, granddad, mum dad and two children. They had a car accident on the way to me and had to cancel. 'Mum' rang me back the next day to tell me the whole disastrous story. Two weeks earlier she had written off her company car when she swerved to avoid a rabbit and put the car through a stone wall. She had whiplash injuries and bruises from the side air bag. The company hired her a car and she insured it for her father (granddad) to drive as well. On their way to me granddad had braked on the wet road and skidded into her and her family, who had in turn, skidded into the car in front. As a consequence she had three insurance claims for three accidents in three different cars in her name in two weeks. If that isn't bad luck I really don't know what is. Also it was bad luck for me as I had lost a good booking.

CHAPTER 18
BUILDERS

Builders where regular visitors to Greenhill and had been since the house was originally built in the late sixteenth century. We could date the original part of the house by the shaping of the beams in the roof and by the fact that the vertical beams downstairs where laid into the ground inside the house but onto large stones on the outside walls. According to the experts the original builders had found out that the wood, if put straight into the ground, would rot and so that is why they were put the beams onto stones at about this time. We did have the local historical people out in the 1980's and they said that, we only had the side rooms off a great hall left and that a window we had taken out of the back was a 'great hall' window which had been reused. Many timbers where reused years ago, the story was that they were originally ship's timbers. They told us that, originally, it would only have been one story high with the fire in the centre of the room rising up to the ceiling and that the upstairs floor would have been added later. In between the timbers we found lathe and plaster with horse hair in it and, in the loft and upstairs we found a panel of mud and straw. We left a section of this in the roof for future generations to see. They didn't know how to list us because a Grade One listing means you can touch nothing without their permission and a Grade Two listing means you can touch nothing outside without their permission. The part of our house which needed protecting was the inside and so as the house wasn't at risk they didn't grade us.

When John's parents had moved to Greenhill in 1945 it had been a house and four flats but the tenants had been moved out in the 1960's as there was no running water in the house and the only toilets were a row of Ty Bach's across the yard. In Welsh Ty Bach translates as 'Little House' but it really means outside toilet. In the 1960's John's parents put running water and a bathroom into their side of the house and used the other half for animals and animal feed. We married in 1970 and did up the empty side to live in. This end was built in stone and, in our kitchen, when the plaster was knocked off, we found the shape of a stable door in the back wall. Fredrick Llewellyn Jones, the Liberal Member of Parliament for Flintshire from 1929 to 1935, lived in the house in the early 1900's and I was lucky enough to speak to his daughter before she died. She told me that they used that room as a stable for their horse but that they had to move nearer to Flint so that her father could catch the London train more easily after he became a Member of Parliament. As part of the improvement process we knocked down two rooms off the end of the house. We later found out that these had been where the barley had been malted when it was an inn in the 1700's. A gentleman arrived up one day saying that he had lived in this end piece as a child and had come back after the war as his father had just died and he had to sort out his affairs. John's parents remembered him and they reminisced about old times. He stayed the night for old time's sake, obviously not in the same rooms but he was thrilled to think he could stay just one more time as he now lived in Australia and was on holiday in the UK.

We surmise that when the 'Great Hall was taken down the room we called the dining room was built. The timbers on the wall between them and the oldest part of the house where rotten and we faced both sides of that wall with plasterboard as it wasn't fit to expose and needed support. This centre room had been built in brick with a semi-circular bay window at the front which had a lead roof. There were no foundations under this and so it was sinking, it was so bad that you couldn't stand a table up in the room and so in the winter of 1979 John and our farm worker, Eddie decided to take it down and rebuild it. That room had a deep fireplace protruding into the room and, as the bricks where rotten we decided to take it down, what we found behind it was four more fireplaces built in rotten brick put one in front of the other. The whole wall was so bad that it was decided to reinforce it with a block wall back filled with concrete. One cold February morning John and Eddie, not knowing if the walls had been interlinked, propped up the walls on either side of the bay and knocked it out along with the fireplace. They built up a four-layer block wall to support the fireplace wall and the next day they filled it with cement to bind it to the rotten bricks. The following day they did the same while at the same time rebuilding the outside wall in block after making foundations and reducing the bay to a straight line. That night the weather forecast was for snow in the next few days and so they built up a layer of eight blocks which took the wall up to the second story. The following day they, again, back filled it with cement. Later in the morning I went up to make the beds in the girl's bedroom, adjacent to the repair work, and found that the wall was bulging in! Boards and planks where found to push the wall back until the cement had set and the girls had to sleep that night with this contraption in place. It did the trick; you can now only see a bulge if you know what you're looking for, it just looks like bad plastering. When the building work in the middle was finished it gave us four more usable rooms, two downstairs and two upstairs. We were able to make the downstairs back room into a small sitting room to give us privacy from the guests who used the front sitting room. It gave us two more bedrooms upstairs, one of which we used as that one opened up onto a landing which hadn't been renovated. The other was a big family room in which we put a shower, washbasin double bed and bunk beds. Years later we altered this room again to add a full ensuite bathroom built in pine with pine fitted wardrobe and dressing table to match. This room then took a double and single bed. The big downstairs room was to be the dining room, but I wanted it to look special. We hunted high and low and eventually bought a second-hand block floor which came out of a school in Whitchurch, Shropshire. We found someone locally who could fit it for us and he did a wonderful job. It was so sad that within eighteen months of him doing the job be died while playing football, it turned out he had one of these unusual heart problems which sometimes strikes young people. I then wanted to have the room panelled as I remembered being impressed by the panelling in my uncle's house, Hankelow Hall in Cheshire. We looked everywhere for second hand panelling without success. A lot of chapels where being stripped out at that time but we couldn't find enough panelling to do the job. Eventually we had it made by a company called Fron Furniture who made reproduction oak furniture at that time. It was their first £1,000 job and it was just the job we wanted. They left the date carved into the panelling, it was 1982. They also provided the oak mantle piece for the guest's front room three years later.

It was fashionable in the early nineteen eighties to have 'Bullseye' window panes in small, windows and so we had three or four put into the dinning room window. Twenty years later we regretted it. Guest would ask us why we had 'Bullseye' panes, especially the Americans or Europeans who had never seen them before. I did get rather tired of having to explain that we had put them in because they were the fashion of the day. The Dinning room was easy to keep clean, I waxed the floor twice a year and the panelling once a year and the top, above the four-foot high panels, was emulsion painted about every six years as it kept so clean. The only exception was when Susan and Jennifer had a party and we found out that Coca Cola strips polish. It took eight tins of polish to bring it back up to its former glory but, give them their due, Sue, Jen and their friends polished it all.

In the late 1980's we got a bank loan to do up the rest of the house after John's parents moved into a bungalow. It was altered specifically as a guest house. Due to the recession at the time our local builder couldn't sell the houses on the small estate he was building and was glad of another job to see him through until times improved. The bank manager had never agreed a loan for a guest house before but I was able to show him the account we had so far and he took a chance on us especially as he was a friend of the builder and knew he needed the work. The bank manager moved on to run a bank in Llandudno and told us what he learned from us helped him deal with the Llandudno hotels and guest houses. Cliff the builder and his team moved in in the autumn and we took bookings on rooms which were not finished for the following spring. It was a nerve-racking time especially when the plumber went on holiday abroad and got a bug which stopped him working. In the end

Cliff had to find another plumber. We used up all sorts of Cliff's left-over goods from his builder's yard to keep the cost down. This meant we had a bedroom with a red bathroom suite, one with a green washbasin and one with a brown washbasin. We just decorated the rooms accordingly and I set to making curtains with material from Abakan. The first job was for all the old plaster to be knocked off the walls; we reckoned they knocked about twenty to twenty-five tons of rubble out of the house before they started. The room that John's parents had made into a bathroom turned out to be hiding an inglenook fireplace full of rubble. There was a fireplace in the half cellar under it and one in the room above as well. The back wall to that room was timber framed and only one brick thick. When they knocked the plaster off the wall it all fell out onto the yard leaving a huge hole. This happened on a Friday afternoon and they had to come back on the Saturday to build up the hole as, being winter, the weather wasn't good.

By the spring we were up and running but alterations never really finished as needs change and we can truthfully say we are experts at moving furniture. That was never an easy task as the stairs on our side of the house went straight up to a T junction with landings right and left neither of which was more than thirty-six inches wide but we did manage to get a three-setter sofa around into one of the bedrooms once. On the guest side the stairs had a half landing and then a turn at the top. All double wardrobes had to be dismantled to move anywhere.

We mustn't finish this chapter without mentioning Keith Harrison, our trusty joiner who, over many years has come to Greenhill to do all sorts of jobs both inside and out. With a smile on his face he has always been able to make one of our ideas work for us and come up with many an ingenious way of getting around the problem of our crooked walls and keeping our house in good order.

Also, our painter, Ian, who we booked to come the first week in January every year to maintain the property in tip top condition. I had worked out that if we painted three rooms a year every room would get painted once every seven years and I had a spread sheet on the computer so that I could remember where wanted painting next. Ian could paint far faster than we could especially the small window panes of which he could paint fifty an hour. Every second year he would come and paint two sides of the outside of the house and then the following year two more sides. He was so relieved that the spaces between the inside ceiling beams would fit his paint roller which saved him having to use a brush which would have been a lot slower. He wasn't so pleased when Susan and Jennifer wanted to paint their bedroom bright pink, well they were girls weren't they. He complained that the pink stained his roller for a long time afterwards. This was made worse when Clare wanted a bright red and yellow bedroom.

CHAPTER 19
OUR GUEST BOOK AND THANKYOU LETTERS.

It took me a long time to read through the guest book and look at all the thank you messages; I don't think I had done that as a whole before. It brought back so many memories and a tear to my eye as I read all the kind messages from our guests and I'm so glad that I could make so many peoples stay a happy one. I also hadn't realised how many nationalities had stayed in our home. I've already mentioned a few but I also found:

Dutch, Belgium, Rhodesian, Manx (Isle of Man), Denmark, Finland, Norway, Trinidadian, Zimbabwean, Israeli, Icelandic, South African, Italian, Japanese, (these guests had children with Beatrix Potter books translated into Japanese) Singaporean, Malaysian, British Chinese, Jamaican, Portuguese, Chilean, Thailand, Luxembourg, Hong Kong, Brazil, Kenya, Colombian, Tenerife, and Spanish guests who had signed our book over the years.

We have had some wonderful messages and thank you letters and I would like to share a few with you:

Our first entry was by Stephen Hains and Mary Force on 8th January 1975 made in a small book we first used before setting up a bigger book which we filled and we eventually started a third book.

July 1975 Mark Kroske also from USA, wrote; 'Enjoyed the hospitality and the milking.

On 11th March 1979 Sylvia, Saad, Gerard and Beruard from France were the first to write on that years page; 'The first for 1979. If following people find the same family and the same bacon they surely won't be deceived!'

14th July 1980 brought Frank and Mary Wattam form Northampton who wrote; 'Very hospitable, don't work too hard. May you prosper?

10th July 1981 Dr. & Mrs D. Haydon Jones wrote; 'It was a happy choice that we came here. Thank you for your cheerful service and the good food.'

And on 15th August we entertained Major Carl J. 'Rusty' Hubbard 3rd and his family from Birmingham, Alabama USA, stationed at RAF Alconbury, Huntingdon, Cambridge. Saying 'First trip and lodging at B&B in Wales with Grandpa Hubbard on Holiday from USA. Outstanding hospitality and perfectly lovely beginning and ending to our trip. Recommend to anyone, Thanks.'

13th September 1982 Terry, Jean, Micheal and David Tarr said; 'This lovely farmhouse was the perfect base for our whirlwind tour of North Wales. We especially enjoyed the cheerful hospitality.'

Skipping on to 21st June 1986 The Vinson family from Surrey was so happy that the children didn't want to go home.

19th July David and Carol Chinaloy originally from China, living in the USA where 'comfortable and cosy, relaxing in a homely atmosphere.'

17th September 1988 was a return visit for Barry Mitan from Tallahassee, USA in fact they said, '3rd year, super as always, I plan my annual UK visits around my visits to your farm – best accommodation in Britain.'

A simple message left 23rd March 1992 was left by Carol and Michael Cook from Sydney, Australia; 'Thank you for sharing your home with us'.

The Rocare Lads from Bournemouth said on 3rd September 1993; 'Only the best will do and we found it.'

10th April 1997 the Stuart's arrive and left with the message; 'Glad we climbed the hill, a very nice ascent, three most enjoyable days, so well spent.'

And on 21st July Athol and Margaret Black from Australia made a second visit with the comment; 'Just as enjoyable, Thank you Mary and John'.

On 23rd July 1997 we have some interesting comments from an Israeli family. I just wish we could translate it!

Followed by Jo and Ben Browne on 30th July with;' At first sight this place looks excellent, but the truth is now out – it's superb!'

On 30th September 1997 an official looking letter arrive which turned out to be from BDC Engineering Services, Dave Bumby and crew to me. I must quote this letter in full as it so moved me:

Many thanks once again for the warm hospitality extended to my colleagues and

myself during our recent visit to your farm accommodation.
It is good to see that you are continually upgrading your facilities. After a hard days work it is a pleasure to return to a clean, homely base with a warm welcome.
We would particularly like to commend you on your meals – they are always imaginative, well presented, of copious supply and always served with a smile.

22nd February 1998 Joyce and Alan Pusser from Leicester said that at last they had found a place in North Wales they could call home.

Another visit for Peter and Allison Williams from Wetherby where happy to say; 'Once again an excellent stay, your breakfast's really do set us up for the day. Thank you'.

24th April 1999 brought Rachael Jones from Powys who was impressed with the attention to detail e.g. items in the bathrooms for emergency and emergency torch behind the bedroom doors'.

4th May 2000 came Bev and Henry Bingham from Australia who were so pleased with all the extras and the use of the washing machine and who also had a most comfortable stay.

On 1st September 2001 our book gained a row of smiley faces followed by 'yepper I liked it!!!!, this was from H. F. Weighelt 3rd from Chicago now living in Germany.

30th May 2003 brought the comment; 'Unique, interesting, lovely – thank you' from chuck and Susanna Salmon from Vancouver Island, Canada.

19th May 2007 came with Gwyn and Richard Sewal from Maine, USA saying; 'What a treat to be here, Wonderful, Wonderful, Thank You'.

There are just far too many wonderful comments in our Guest Book and the last one came from Caroline and David from Lincoln on 14th September 2011 with the words; 'A lovely welcome. Good luck for the future. Enjoy your retirement.

On 19th November 2011 we had a farm sale at which we also sold most of the furniture from the guest house and on 25th November we moved into our bungalow about five miles from the farm where I am writing this from.

Although running a guest house and farm was very hard work with some long hours we have so many happy memories and have made some wonderful friends, but it was time to move on and let someone younger take up the reins although the farm is not now run as a guest house it is still a big house to take care of. We hope that it will survive for another four hundred years if successive owners give it the love and attention we gave it. It is the least it deserves for looking after so many families over the years and giving them all such happy memories.

What more can you ask of a house?

21290153R00161

Printed in Great Britain
by Amazon